Come, Let Us Reason

Come, Let Us Reason

An Introduction to Logical Thinking

Norman L. Geisler
and
Ronald M. Brooks

 **BAKER BOOK HOUSE**
Grand Rapids, Michigan 49516

Copyright © 1990 by Baker Books
a division of Baker Book House Company
P.O. Box 6287, Grand Rapids, MI 49516-6287

ISBN: 0-8010-3836-7

Fifth printing, July 1998

Printed in the United States of America

Library of Congress Cataloging–in–Publication Data
Geisler, Norman L.
    Come, let us reason: an introduction to logical thinking/Norman L.
Geisler and Ronald M. Brooks.
        p.   cm.
    Includes bibliographical references and index.
    ISBN 0-8010-3836-7
    1. Logic. 2. Philosophy and religion. I. Brooks, Ronald M. (Ronald
Matthew), 1957– . II. Title.
    BC108.G331990
    160—dc20   90–38822
                                                              CIP

For information about academic book, resources for Christian leaders, and
all new releases available from Baker Book House, visit our web site:
                    http://www.bakerbooks.com/

Contents

Preface

God is rational, and he has created us as rational beings. The Bible urges us to give the reason for the hope that is in us (1 Pet. 3:15, NIV). Indeed, Jesus declared that the greatest commandment is: "You shall love the Lord your God with all . . . your mind" (Matt. 22:37). The apostle Paul added, "whatever is true, . . . think on . . ." (Phil. 4:8). Thinking is not an option for the Christian; it is an imperative.

Of course, everyone thinks. But not everyone thinks correctly. The name of the discipline that is geared to correcting this problem is logic. The late professor Gordon H. Clark pressed this point when he boldly, if not entirely accurately, translated John 1:1 this way: "In the beginning was Logic [the *Logos*]. And Logic was with God, and Logic was God." Of course, God is more than a rational being; he also has feeling and free will. Nonetheless, God is rational, and the principles of good reason do flow from his very nature. Consequently, learning the rules of clear and correct reasoning is more than an academic exercise. For the Christian, it is also a means of spiritual service.

I am personally indebted to my first logic teacher, Howard Schoof. His exhortation seems more appropriate as the years roll by: "The next best thing besides godliness for a Christian is logic." Clean living and correct thinking make a potent combination. In short, we should get our life cleaned up on the outside and our thinking cleared up on the inside.

The need for clear and correct thinking has not diminished with time. With the infiltration of New Age thinking into our culture, there is an increased emphasis on feeling over thinking, on the subjective over the objective. Shirley MacLaine, pop theologian of the New Age movement, was surely out on a limb when she wrote: "Don't evaluate and don't let your left brain judge what you are thinking. Give your left brain more space. As a matter of fact, don't think" (*Dancing in the Light*, 312). It is hard to think of worse advice. It is one of our purposes in writing this book to correct this kind of nonthinking.

There are, of course, many other books available on how to think. (Some of them are listed in the Bibliography.) Why another? First, there are few directed at Christians. Further, many available books go right over the head of the average person. Finally, none use theological and apologetic illustrations throughout. This book is different in all these ways. I hope this invitation to good thinking will dawn like the morning sun, burning away some of the fog created by a feeling-dominated culture.

—Norman L. Geisler

In the summer before my freshman year of college I began reading a book that changed my life. It was Aristotle's *Prior Analytics*, his text on logic. As I sat in the courtyard of an abandoned dormitory, his thoughts gave me the structure that I had been missing in my own attempts to understand the world. Eighteen months later I found myself entering a church service and the first words I heard were those of Isaiah 1:18, "Come, now, let us reason together . . . Though your sins are as scarlet they will be as white as snow." That morning I came face to face with the stark reality that the faith which I had repudiated and reviled was indeed the truth, and I became a Christian.

God and I have done a great deal of reasoning together since then. Though my spiritual life certainly has not been void of emotionalism and fits of both rigor and contrition, the most dramatic changes in me—and those that I find most liberating—have been intellectual transformations. Paul anticipated this when he defined discipleship as "the renewing of your mind" (Rom. 12:2) and called for "destroying speculations . . . taking every thought captive to the obedience of Christ" (2 Cor. 10:5). If, after all, angels are pure intellect and we are in spiritual warfare with them, then it must be a battle of ideas. This book should be considered basic training for that battle, for herein lie the keys to discernment.

A special thanks to Drs. Richard Owlsley, Anthony Damico, and Jake Kobler for introducing me to Aristotle, logic, and discernment, for these lead me to the Truth.

—Ronald M. Brooks

Acknowledgments

Without the help of many others this book would not be possible. Special thanks is due to Drs. Phil West and Richard Howe, both logic teachers, who made many helpful additions. Likewise, E. Calvin Beisner made a significant contribution in editing the manuscript. In addition, our thanks go to Mark Foreman, who wrote the exercises, appendix, glossary, and indexes; and to our office staff: Sharon Coomer, Terry Hayden, and Chris Coomer, who together collated the index. The book is much improved as a result of their efforts.

1

The Whats and Whys of Logic

It is the function of the wise man to know
order.—Aristotle

What is logic? And why in the world would anyone want to
study it? Isn't it just a bunch of incomprehensible and arbitrary
rules that no one really follows anyway? What good does it do?
To most people, logic is an unknown language about an
unknown realm, where everything is turned upside down and
no one with an IQ below 300 is allowed. You can see it in the
panic on their faces when you just mention the word—*LOGIC*!
    Despite all the bad press, logic is not so tough. In fact, it is one
of the simplest things to use because you use it all the time,
though you may not realize it. We don't mean that you put all
of your thoughts into logical form and do a formal analysis of
each thought. But when you are at the supermarket and one
brand of sugar is 3 cents per ounce but another is 39 cents per
pound, it doesn't take long for you to pull out your calculator
and settle the issue. Why do you do that? Because you recognize that those ounces and pounds have to be put in the same
category to be compared. That's logic. You use logic to do 'most
everything. When you decide to take your shower after you
work out instead of before, you don't necessarily go through all
the formal steps it takes to reach that conclusion validly, but
your decision rests on logic nonetheless. *Logic really means putting
your thoughts in order.*

What Is Logic?

Order is the key word. It applies to all kinds of different disciplines. In *nature*, there is an order that reason discovers but does not produce. The patterns of quartz crystals, the regularity of natural laws, the movements of the planets, the complex information in a single strand of DNA—all these show us an order that we can see but that we did nothing to put there, just as you can read this book, but you didn't put the words on the pages.

In *art*, however, we do produce order. The artist, whether a painter, sculptor, composer, actor, or writer, imposes order on the things around him. He crafts the lines he wants to see. He bends the steel to suit his purpose. He arranges the rhythms, the melodies, and the harmonies to express a certain feeling. Art is created by a person imposing order on the things of the external world.

In *philosophical* thinking there is order also. *Ethical* order is order that reason produces in acts of the will. In other words, it is the ordering of our thoughts about the right and wrong of the things we choose. That doesn't mean that there is no absolute right or wrong; it only means that the way we think about it is something that we produce. Whenever we ask a question about what we *ought* to do, we are ordering our choices by an ethical standard. That order tells us what we really think is good. It shows us what our values really are. Should I lie to save twenty bucks? Should I help the lady stranded on the freeway, or hurry home to watch football? How we answer depends on an ethical order that we produce about the choices we make. The best system of ethics is the one that best expresses the way things ought to be, i.e., what really is good and valuable.

The order of *logic* is very similar. It, too, is an ordering that we produce, but it is concerned with ordering our thoughts. Logic is reason looking at itself to see how good reason works. It studies the methods that we use to analyze information and draw valid conclusions. It puts all of these methods into an order that gives us the right way to draw conclusions. The best system of logic is the one that is best suited to drawing proper conclusions from the premises.

To state this as a formal definition we might say, *"Logic is the study of right reason or valid inferences and the attending fallacies, formal and informal."* If you are reading this book for a class, no doubt that is the definition your teacher will make you memorize. Let's break it up and simplify it some.

Logic is the study of right reason. . . . That is the main point. Logic is a study, an ordering, of how to think rightly, or how to find truth. Paraphrasing this, we might say, *logic is a way to think so that we come to correct conclusions.*

. . . **or valid inferences.** . . . That means *implications*. Part of studying logic is recognizing when A implies B and when it does not. There are clear-cut rules to help us with this.

. . . **and the attending fallacies, formal and informal.** A fallacy is a *mistake*. Sometimes we make mistakes in the way we set up our thinking, or by using an implication that is not true. These are called formal fallacies, because they have to do with the form of the argument (more about that later). Other times the mistakes are in the meanings of the terms we use. They might be unclear or misleading. Or, they might just not have anything to do with the subject at hand. Mistakes like these are called informal fallacies. Knowing the kinds of mistakes we can make helps us to avoid them.

If we put all of our paraphrases together, we get a simplified definition: *Logic is a way to think so that we can come to correct conclusions by understanding implications and the mistakes people often make in thinking.*

Why Study Logic?

Simply put, you can't avoid studying logic, so you might as well know what you're doing. It is the basis for all other studies. It is the basis for all math and science. Even music, from Bach to the Beach Boys, is based on logic. Without it, there could be no rational discussion of anything; writing would be impossible. How can you put a sentence together without a logical order?

Even interpretation requires logic. We have to assume that the author tried to communicate a logical thought, and the only way we have to find that thought is to put all the clues together and set them in logical order. This is as true for English literature as for Bible study. Biblical theology and systematic theology involve imposing an order on the data of their fields. And giving a reason for your faith would be useless if it were not a logical reason that you expected others to accept on rational grounds. The only way to avoid logic is to quit thinking, because logic is the basis for all thought.

Now, there are lots of complaints about studying logic, especially as it applies to God. So before we go any farther, we'd better clear the air and answer some of those questions, which, if you haven't heard yet, you will hear someday.

There are many kinds of logic. Why choose only Aristotelian (Western) logic? True, there are other kinds of logic that we might study, and maybe you will go on to read about non-Aristotelian logic, but the basic laws of logic are the same for all logic. They are necessary and undeniable, not just arbitrary rules that someone made up. Aristotle didn't *invent* logic; he only helped to *discover* it. These undeniable laws are the same for all thinking; once you know them, you can go on to look at other kinds of philosophies.

People are not logical. Why bother? Often people are not moral either; does that mean that we should close down all the churches and fire the police force? People may not act morally, but they *ought* to; and we should use every means to teach them how and remind them of proper behavior. Likewise, people may not think logically at times, but still, they *ought* to. If logic is a way to think so that we find truth, then we always ought to be logical so that we know the truth.

Logic doesn't work. People don't respond to it. Logic does work on reasonable people, and everyone should be reasonable. On unreasonable people, nothing works. So why not try to be reasonable and let the other fellow be unreasonable? Besides, something is not true or right because it works. The idea that it is, is called pragmatism. If you were taking a true/false exam and wrote for your answer to one question, "It works," what would the teacher do? Whether it works or not is a totally different question from whether it is true or false. It has nothing to do with true and false, or right and wrong. All it tells you is that it works. If that is the criterion for truth, then you could never know that anything was true unless you knew that every time you tried it in the future it would work. Can you imagine a witness taking the stand in a courtroom and pledging "to tell the expedient, the whole expedient, and nothing but the expedient, so help me future experience"? Pragmatism is no test for truth.

Not everything is subject to logic. That is true. Only questions of truth are subject to logic. Logic gives us rules for rational judgments and inferences, but it says nothing about some kinds of statements. For example, it says nothing about emotive expressions, that is, expressions of feelings. When you touch a hot stove and say, "Ouch," that expression is neither true nor false.

It is simply an expression of your feeling. A housewife in tears over the way her preschoolers have abused her all day is totally in the realm of the subjective, and logic has nothing to do with the way she feels. Of course, we could make logical statements about the way she feels, like, "She either feels bad or she doesn't." But her emotive outburst, "Good grief!" is neither true nor false and is not subject to logic. Likewise, aesthetic expressions are not true or false. They are beautiful. They are to be appreciated, not analyzed. Moral judgments are right or wrong, not true or false. No one asks, "Is abortion true or false?" That is like asking, "What does blue smell like?" True/false categories don't fit everything. However, logic can evaluate the consistency between moral judgments and the inferences from them. It can help us understand some things even about areas that it can't enter into.

Logic is contrary to human intuitions. Not necessarily. Intuition can be a source of truth, but once a person makes a claim about his intuitions, it can be tested by the laws of logic. Suppose George's intuition tells him that this is a great night to sit down and read the newspaper after dinner. Meanwhile, George's wife intuits that it is time for George to start contributing something to the household chores and that he should come wash the dishes. Both intuitions cannot be true; the law of noncontradiction tells us that quite plainly. The ensuing battle suggests that they both may be wrong. Intuition can be true, but you can't *know* that it is true until you make some claim about it that can be tested with the laws of logic.

Logic and God

One of the objections to studying logic most often cited is that logic does not apply to God or to any of the mysteries of the Christian faith, such as the Trinity or the Incarnation. If that were true, then logic might be of use in natural science and things in this world, but it would be useless in finding the truth about God. In other words, logic would apply to temporal, finite reality, but not to ultimate reality. Some Christians really believe this. We don't. Why? Because even those who claim, "Logic does not apply to God," use logic in that very statement. Logic is unavoidable.

Theology is a *logos* about the *theos*—the logic of God. Theology is a rational discourse about God. The Gospel of John begins

with the statement, "In the beginning was the *Logos.*" The basis
of all logic is that some statements are true and others are false.
If this word about God is not a logical word, then what is it? The
whole idea of theology is that rational statements can be made
about God. Even someone who says the opposite has just made
a rational (although untrue) statement about God. Logic is
undeniable.

Logic is built on four undeniable laws. There is no "getting
behind" these laws to explain them. They are self-evident and
self-explanatory. There is also no way around them. In order to
reject any of these statements, one must assume the very principle he seeks to deny. But if you must assume that something is
true to say that it is false, you haven't got a very good case, have
you?

For example, the *law of non-contradiction* (A is not non-A) says
that no two contradictory statements can both be true at the
same time and in the same sense. Now, if someone tried to deny
this and said, "The law of non-contradiction is false," he would
have a problem. Without the law of noncontradiction, there is
no such thing as true or false, because this law itself draws the
line between true and false. So we can't call it false without
assuming that it is true. The same thing happens when someone
tries to deny the other laws: the *law of identity* (A is A), the *law
of excluded middle* (either A or non-A), and the *law of rational
inference.*

Theological method builds on the foundation of these ele-
mentary laws of logic. If logic is a necessary precondition of all
thought, then it must also be necessary for all thought about
God.

If the law of noncontradiction were not true, then theological
paradox would be inevitable. We would never be able to say
about God, "This is true and that is false." Our thoughts about
him would be a continuous series of contradictions without any
real affirmations. Without the law of identity, theological unity
would be unachievable. We would wrangle forever without
realizing that we already had agreement.

Unless valid inferences can be made from what is known to
what is unknown, there can be no theological argumentation.
Whether in a discussion between Christians on a matter of
interpretation or in a debate with a non-Christian, no one could
prove any point without the laws of rational inference. These
tools of the theologian are all kept in the logician's toolbox.

From the standpoint of reality, we understand that God is the basis of all logic. As the ultimate reality, all truth is ultimately found in him. He has created the reality that we know and in which we have discovered the laws of logic. Even Jesus said, "I am . . . the truth" (John 14:6). He has structured the world in such a way that these laws cannot be denied; however, we did not know God first and then learn logic from him. He exists as the basis of all logic (in reality), but we discovered logic first and came to know God through it. This is true even if we came to know God through his revelation, because we understood the revelation through logic. In the order of being, God is first; but in the order of knowing, logic leads us to all knowledge of God. God is the basis of all logic (in the order of *being*), but logic is the basis of all knowledge of God (in the order of *knowing*).

Objections to Logic in Theology

Just as some object to studying logic, there are also those who decry the use of logic in theology. In fact, using logic in theology is not very popular in some circles. Some theologians revel in "paradox" and "antinomy," as if it were somehow more spiritual to believe in the absurd. However, the objections to using logic seem to be based on misunderstandings. Answering these questions should clarify things.

Using logic puts logic before God. No. We use logic in the process of knowing God, but that does not mean that God came after logic in reality. Without God, nothing could have existence. God is the basis of all logic in reality and he is in no way inferior to logic. Logic comes from God, not God from logic. But when it comes to how we know things, logic is the basis of all thought, and it must come before any thought about anything, including God. For example, I need a map before I can get to Washington, D.C. But Washington must exist before the map can help me get there. Even so, we use logic first to come to know God, but God exists first before we can know him.

Using logic makes God subject to our logic. First, it isn't *our* logic. Man didn't invent logic, he only discovered it. God is the author of all logic. So, technically speaking, God does not flow from logic; logic flows from God. Second, it isn't God that we examine using logic; it is our statements about God. No one is trying to judge God. It is the statements that we make about him that we analyze with logic. Logic simply provides a way to see if those statements are true—if they fit with the reality of who God

really is. Finally, in applying logic to those statements, God is
not being tested by some standard outside himself. Logic flows
from God. It is part of his rational nature, which has been given
to us in his image. Using logic in theology is simply applying
God's test to our statements about God. It is God's way for us to
come to the truth.

Using logic is a form of rationalism. Being reasonable and being a
rationalist are quite different. A rationalist tries to determine all
truth by reason. Reasonable Christians only try to discover it. A
rationalist won't let any empirical data change his conclusion;
he doesn't want to be confused by the facts. A reasonable person
takes account of the facts, incorporates them into his views, and
sometimes changes his conclusions when new facts become
known. Further, some rationalists won't even let the Bible
change the conclusions they have reached by reason.

A reasonable person, by contrast, will take contradiction as a
sign that his statement about God is wrong. Rationalists set the
limits of what can be true about God. Reasonable people only
use logic to test the truth of their statements about God.

*The Bible says that God can do the impossible. Doesn't that mean he
is not bound by logical limitations?* God can do what is *humanly*
impossible, but not what is *actually* impossible. Some things are
impossible because of our human limitations, such as walking
through walls, raising the dead, and being in two places at once.
But these things are possible for God, who has no body, is the
giver of life, and is always everywhere. He is not subject to
human limitations. But this does not mean that God can literally
do anything—including what is actually impossible. Hebrews
6:18 says that it is impossible for God to lie. James 1:13 says that
God cannot be tempted, and 2 Timothy 2:13 says that it is
impossible for him to deny his own oath. These things are
impossible for a perfectly good God who cannot do evil.

Neither can God make a square circle, nor a triangle with two
sides; nor can anyone else. Those things can't possibly exist
because they are self-contradictory things. No circle can be a
square because squares have four straight sides and circles don't.
All triangles must have three sides or they aren't triangles. These
things are impossible ideas—you can't even imagine what they
would be. They are *logically* impossible. The same goes for the
mountain so big that God can't move it. How can anything be

too big for the infinite power of God to handle? If God can make it, he can move it.

Teaching this has brought some unusual responses. One student asked, "Is it possible for me to jump over the moon?" The teacher responded, "That's logically possible, if you could get a really good jump and break the earth's gravity. But it is humanly impossible because nobody can jump that way." Certain that God must be able to do something that he can't, the fellow asked, "Well, can God jump over the moon?" He recognized that God should be able to do what is logically possible, even if it is humanly impossible; he just forgot that God is everywhere all the time. God does not need to jump over the moon. He is already over it. God is not a here-or-there type of being, so he can't jump *from* here *to* there. Only later did we realize that the simpler response was to tell the student, "No, God can't jump over the moon because he doesn't have any legs."

If God created the laws of logic, then why can't he break them? After all, he created the laws of nature, and he breaks them every time he does a miracle. There is a big difference between the laws of nature and the laws of logic. Natural law is really only a description of how things normally *do* operate; but laws of logic are more like ethical laws that tell us how our minds *should* operate, even if that is not the way we always think. Natural laws deal with the way things are; logical laws deal with the way things ought to be. In this sense, logical laws are *prescriptive*, calling for our obedience, since we ought to think logically. But natural laws are only *descriptive* and make no such demand. Also, logic flows from God's rational nature, and he cannot change his nature. That would be going against all that he is. It would be betraying himself. It would be like God's breaking a moral law, which also flows from his nature. Can you imagine God being unjust? Or unloving? Then how can you imagine him breaking the laws of logic?

Don't some doctrines, like the Trinity, the incarnation of Christ, and predestination, involve contradictions? In each of these cases, it can be shown that there is no real contradiction involved. Some theologians have used words like *antinomy* or *paradox* to describe the problems encountered in these doctrines, but those words imply a contradiction. Surely these things are mysteries that go *beyond* human reason, and we cannot grasp them fully, but they are not contradictions that go *against* reason.

For example, the doctrine of the Trinity, if understood as saying that God is three persons yet only one person, would be self-contradictory. However, the orthodox doctrine of the Trinity says that there are three persons in one being. There is no self-contradiction in that. We have only seen one person per being with human nature here on earth, but that does not mean that an infinite being with God's nature couldn't exist as more than one person. How it works is beyond us, but it is not a contradiction.

The doctrine of the incarnation would be self-contradictory if it said that Christ had both a human and a divine nature in one *nature*. But it doesn't. We say that Christ had two natures united in one *person*. *Who* Christ is as an individual is the same for both his deity and his humanity, but *what* he is divinely is different from what he is humanly. This is a mystery that has been revealed only partially, but it is not a paradox that cannot be resolved.

Predestination also confuses some people. As a morally perfect being, God cannot *force* free people to do what they do not choose. Furthermore, forced freedom is a contradiction. But it is not contradictory for God to *determine* what people will do with their free choice. In this way, God can control and determine the choices we make, but he does not force those choices on us. God works persuasively, not coercively. We still experience our choices as free—as our decisions—even though God both knew what we would decide and chose that we would decide it long before we did. Forced freedom is a contradiction, but God determinately choosing that I make a free choice is not.

Looking Ahead

Now that we have eliminated those objections to studying logic, "Come, let us reason together." There are two different types of reasoning that we need to study. The first is *deductive* or syllogistic logic. Chapters 2 through 4 deal with that topic. Chapter 5 lists the kinds of errors or formal fallacies that should be avoided in this type of argument. Chapter 6 treats the informal fallacies common to human discourse. Chapter 7 makes all this information more useful by showing a method for converting everyday reading into logical arguments. Chapter 8 introduces *inductive* logic, while chapter 9 focuses on one aspect of induction, the scientific method. chapter 10 cites the fallacies of inductive logic.

2

Building Blocks

Any kid who has played with tinker toys knows that there are lots of different kinds of blocks that go into a windmill or a skyscraper. Some are different sizes; some have different shapes. In some, the difference is only in the angle of the holes. And some pieces may look alike, but they can be used in several different ways. It's the same with logic, only we don't build windmills and skyscrapers; we build arguments. Still, there are a few basic building blocks that we always use. So, just like a child opening his first erector set, we need to look at all the pieces and see what they are and how they fit together and try out every possible combination before we try to build anything.

There are different ways we use this word *argument*. In its popular usage, we often mean an emotional disagreement between two persons. This is what a person usually means when he says, "I had an argument with my wife last night." In this sense, our usual reaction is to avoid arguments. However, that is not its technical meaning in logic. By *argument* we mean simply *the providing of reasons for the basis of a conclusion*. Emotions are not (and should never be) involved at all in this sense of *argument*. In logic we don't avoid arguments, we encourage them. In fact you cannot do good logical thinking without them.

The kind of argument that we want to build, ultimately, is called a syllogism. It is made up of three sentences called propositions. A proposition is what we call a sentence that affirms (or denies) something when we use it in a syllogism. Each proposition is made up of two terms, like a subject and a predicate in grammar. The key to the whole thing is in how the terms relate to one another as

21

they are put together in the premises. In other words, you have to make sure that the building blocks you are using have holes in the right places so that you can fit them together.

Here is one way they are supposed to fit together. The terms we will use are A, B, and C. True, those don't stir any life-changing decisions, but we will use them to represent three categories of things. Now, for a syllogism, we need two premises and a conclusion. Let's be really creative and say:

> Premise #1: All A is inside B.
> Premise #2: All B is inside C.
> Conclusion: All A is inside C.

Wasn't that enlightening? Maybe it would help if you saw a diagram illustrating this syllogism. You'll find one in Figure 2.1.

See how all of A is inside B and all of B is inside C? So naturally all of A is inside C also. To those who expected this to be difficult, we hate to disappoint you, but that's it. The basis of syllogistic reasoning is right in those circles. Things can get more complicated, but when in doubt, draw some circles.

Figure 2.1

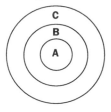

In all fairness, we need to tell you that there is another kind of logic that does not use syllogisms. It is called inductive logic (see chapter 6). A syllogism only has three propositions (two premises and a conclusion), but an inductive argument will have a string of pieces of evidence that may be as long or short as we can imagine. Using syllogisms is called deductive logic because it involves deducing particular conclusions from general statements.[1] In inductive logic, we start with the particulars and reason to general prin-

---

1. We can also deduce universal conclusions from universal statements, as follows: All sinners will die. All men are sinners. Therefore, all men will die. However, a universal cannot be deduced from a particular.

ciples.[2] Deductive logic starts with the cause and reasons to the effect, while inductive logic starts with the effects and attempts to find the cause. That is why deductive reasoning is called *a priori* (*prior* to looking at the facts) and inductive reasoning is called *a posteriori* (*after* seeing the evidence). Syllogisms are more philosophical, and inductive arguments are more scientific. The biggest difference, though, is that deductive arguments yield necessary conclusions (that is, the conclusions are necessarily true if the premises are true and the inferences are valid), but inductive reasoning yields only probable conclusions. The conclusions might have a high degree of probability, but they are still not as certain as deductive conclusions. Figure 2.2 summarizes the differences between deduction and induction.

Figure 2.2

Deduction	Induction
from general to particular	from particular to general
from general to general	from particular to particular
from cause to effect	from effect to cause
a priori reasoning	a posteriori reasoning
philosphical reasoning	scientific reasoning
necessary conclusion	probable conclusion

Truth and Validity

A deductive argument's having the right form does not mean that its conclusion is necessarily true. There is a difference between truth and validity. Validity is the concern of *formal* logic. It deals with how well the argument is put together (its form). Truth concerns *material* logic. It deals with the content of the argument and whether the premises and conclusion correspond to reality. Formal logic can be represented in symbols that have no material meaning, but truth can be found only in meaningful statements.

The difference becomes evident once we start looking at some examples. On the one hand, an argument might be valid (formally) but have one or more false premises:

2. Of course, we can also come to particular conclusions by induction, as follows: Swan one is white. Swan two is white. Swan three is white. Therefore, Swan four is white. The point is that in induction we do not argue from general to particular, as in deduction. Furthermore, the conclusion is not certain even if the premises are true.

All Muslims are holy rollers. (Somehow that doesn't sound
    right.)
All holy rollers are chain smokers. (Not the ones I know!)
Therefore, all Muslims are chain smokers. (I think we missed
    the boat.)

Both premises and the conclusion are false, but formally the
argument is valid. In fact, it is the same as our A, B, and C syllogism with the circles. You can't argue with the circles, but the
content is just not true. You might say that all the building
blocks were in the right place, but the colors clashed. So an
argument can be valid, even if its conclusion is false. Validity
only means that *if* the premises are true, *then* the conclusion
must be also. However, if the premises are not true, then the
conclusion may not be true, even though it is validly drawn
from them.

On the other hand, an argument might have all true premises
and a true conclusion but be formally invalid:

All good angels are part of God's heavenly kingdom. (True)
Gabriel is part of God's heavenly kingdom. (That's what
    Daniel said.)
Therefore, Gabriel is a good angel. (I wouldn't argue for a
    minute.)

What could possibly be wrong with that? Everything about it
is true. The problem is that it has a major loophole in the logic.
Angels are only *part* of God's kingdom. Saved men are there too.
Isn't it possible that Gabriel is a saved man? The circles just don't
fit together. (See Figure 2.3.)

Figure 2.3

We can't throw form out just because we like the conclusion. A good logical argument, usually called a sound argument, is both valid and has true premises. Only then is its conclusion proven.

Categorical Propositions

There are three kinds of statements that can be used as premises in a syllogism: hypothetical, disjunctive, and categorical. The first kind is an "If . . . then" statement, which we call a conditional or hypothetical proposition. But that is not what we want to talk about now. Another kind is the type that disjoins things by an "either . . . or . . ." We don't want to talk about that either. Let's file both of these away until we learn how syllogisms work.

Figure 2.4

Three Kinds of Propositions

1. Hypothetical—"*If* this, *then* that."
2. Disjunctive—"Either this *or* that."
3. Categorical—"This *is* that."

The third kind, the kind that we do want to talk about, is called a categorical proposition. It is a simple statement that either affirms or denies something. It just says "yes" or "no" about something. When a politician gets caught with his hand in the covert operations fund, he usually says, "I deny the charges categorically," meaning that he flatly rejects their truth in part and in whole. That is, he denies that he should be placed in the category of crooks. A categorical proposition is a "black is black" and "white is white" type of statement, no ifs, ands, or buts about it.

There are four parts to any categorical proposition: the subject term, the predicate term, the copula, and quantifiers. Are you beginning to have flashbacks of high school grammar? These parts are really just identifying the grammatical parts of the sentence.

1. The Subject term—the thing or thought about which the assertion is made.
2. The Predicate term—that which is asserted about the subject term.

3. The copula—that which joins the subject and predicate terms (*is* or *is not*).
4. Quantifiers—the extent or number of the subject (all, some, none).

To put it another way, there are four elements: *what* you're talking about (subject), what you're *saying* about it (predicate), an "is" or "is not" to *connect* them (copula), and *how much* of it you are referring to (quantifier). When we put the four parts together, they look like this:

Quantifier Subject *Copula* Predicate

All A *is* B

If you ever had one of those English teachers who made you diagram sentences, she undoubtedly would have asked you to use the pattern shown in Figure 2.5 to construct a categorical proposition. The proposition "All humans are mortal" tells us about humans. It affirms that they (subject) are (copula—a form of the verb *to be*) mortal (predicate adjective). The extent or number of humans to whom this applies is said to be "all" (quantifier). The same form works on all kinds of subjects, though.

"All flesh is grass. . . ." [Isa. 40:6]
". . . some of those who are standing here shall not taste death until they see the Son of Man coming in His kingdom." [Matt. 16:28]
No "fornicators, nor idolaters, nor adulterers, . . . nor homosexuals, . . . shall inherit the kingdom of God." [1 Cor. 6:9–10]

See? Categorical propositions are all over the place, and they all follow the same pattern.

Figure 2.5

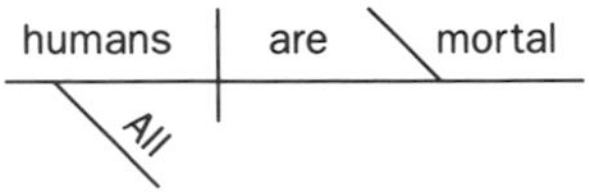

By the way, subject and predicate are not interchangeable. The copula is not like an equal sign in math, where the two sides can be switched. The Mad Hatter and March Hare explain this well:

> "Then you should say what you mean," the March Hare went on.
> "I do," Alice hastily replied; "at least—at least I mean what I say—that's the same thing, you know."
> "Not the same thing a bit!" said the Hatter. "Why, you might as well say that 'I see what I eat' is the same thing as 'I eat what I see'!"
> "You might just as well say," added the March Hare, "that 'I like what I get' is the same thing as 'I get what I like'!"
> "You might just as well say," added the Dormouse, "that 'I breathe when I sleep' is the same thing as `I sleep when I breathe'!"
> "It *is* the same thing with you," said the Hatter.[3]

Quality and Quantity

As we have seen, the subject and predicate change the content of a proposition, but not its basic pattern. But changing the copula and the quantifiers can make a significant difference in the pattern of categorical propositions. How much difference? When we change "is" to "is not," or "some" to "all," that is very significant. These differences are called quality (when we change the copula) and quantity (when we change the quantifiers).

The copula of any proposition can be either positive or negative. It can either affirm or deny the relation between the subject and the predicate. It can say "is" or "is not," "was" or "was not," "will be" or "will not be." The tense does not matter, just the affirming or negating factor. We call these qualities *affirmative* or *negative*. If the proposition says "All men are sinners," it is affirmative. For that matter, the sentence "It is affirmative" is affirmative. If we say, "God is not a man" (Num. 23:19), our proposition is negative.

Watch out! There is a trick to these things. If that sentence were changed to "God is non-man," it would become affirmative, even though it means the same thing. Look closely. The quality of a proposition depends on what is stated in the copula. "Non-man" is in the predicate, not the copula. The statement affirms that God is truly in the category of non-human things. The net result may be the same, but the way of saying it is different. If S stands for subject and P stands for predicate, an affirmative proposition may take the form "S is P" or "S is non-P."

The same thing is true for negative propositions. "Circles are not squares" is negative, but so is "No circles are squares." I know, the "No" looks like a quantifier, not a copula. This is one of those oddities of language where "No circles are squares" means "Circles are not squares" or "All circles are non-squares." For practical purposes, just remember this: No *and* not *go with the copula and* non- *and* un- *go with subjects and predicates. So a negative proposition may have the form "S is not P" or "No S is P."*

Turning our attention to the quantifiers, we find that they can make a proposition either universal (all) or particular (some). We only look at the quantifier on the subject; the predicate usually won't have one. If the proposition refers to all things that can be included in the subject, it is called *universal*. Universal propositions generally have the word *All* or *No* at the beginning. If the proposition refers to only part of the subject group, it is called *particular*. Propositions of this kind start with words like *some* and *not all*. If no quantifier is given, then we assume that the proposition is universal. Now, universal does not mean that it applies to the whole universe; it only means that it applies to all that is in the category defined by the subject. The subject "all matter" may cover a vast number of members, but the number of members in the subject "Socrates" is one. Both are universal, though, because both refer to all in their categories. Likewise, "some" is indefinite and may refer to 99.999 percent of its members or to "at least one," but it always means less than all. Here are examples of the form and content of universal and particular propositions:

Universal propositions: *All S is P,* or *No S is P.*
"All men have sinned."
"None is righteous, no, not one."
Particular propositions: *Some S is P,* or *Some S is not P.*
"Some seed was scattered among the weeds."
"But there are some of you who do not believe."

Four Types of Propositions

We have seen that categorical propositions vary by quality (affirmative or negative, governed by the copula) and quantity (universal or particular, governed by the quantifier). These variations comprise four types of propositions that we can designate with single letters. We arrive at these four types of propositions simply by combining the two qualities with the two quantities. Both affirmative and negative statements can be either universal or particular. We designate the resulting four options as follows:

Type A: Universal affirmative: All S is P and S is P
Type E: Universal negative: No S is P and S is not P
Type I: Particular affirmative: Some S is P
Type O: Particular negative: Some S is not P

These four types exhaust all the possibilities. There can be no other kind of categorical proposition. If you can think of some other kind of logical statement, it is not categorical. It is either hypothetical (If . . . then) or disjunctive (either . . . or).

The advantage to giving these names to types of propositions is that we can write the form of a syllogism in shorthand by just saying what type of propositions it has for its premises and conclusion. As we will see later, once we know the valid forms, this shorthand can tell us if the syllogism is valid or not. Besides, it is much more convenient to use single letters than to recite constantly all of those particular affirmatives and negative universals. In this way, we can refer to both quality and quantity with one easy name.

Sometimes, universal statements can be stated a little differently, so be alert. "All S is P" and "S is P" are both type A statements, because *all* is implied whenever it is not stated. When *all* is stated, the proposition is called *general*; when it is omitted, the proposition is called *individual*. Negative universals (type E) also are designated as general and individual, depending on where the negative is stated. If it is placed before the subject (as in "No S is P") then the proposition is general. Remember that the word *No* here is still part of the copula. If the negative is stated with the copula (S is not P), then the proposition is individual. This difference will have no effect on our shorthand and does not apply to particular statements (types I and O).

In order to avoid confusion, a universal negative should be stated as "No S is P" and not as "All S are not P." Statements that use the form "All . . . are not . . ." are confusing because in our normal usage, when we say "All . . . are not . . ." we often mean "Some . . . are not . . . ." Look at this example: "All dogs are not friendly." When we really think about what we are saying here, it's not, "No dogs are friendly" (universal negative). What we really mean is, "Some dogs are not friendly." Therefore, in order to avoid this confusion, a universal negative proposition should be stated in the form "No . . . is . . ." and not "All . . . are not. . . ."

Distribution of Terms

So far we have said that every syllogism is made up of propositions, and every proposition is made up of two terms, a subject and a predicate. These terms are related to one another by copulas and quantifiers, so that there are four possible types of propositions. Now we want to talk about the terms as we find them in those four types of statements.

Categorical syllogisms always deal with placing things in the categories where they belong, so it is important to know when we are talking about all of a category and when we are talking about only part of it. We covered this for the subjects in our propositions when we discussed quantity. Subjects in universal propositions refer to all in that category (All men have a worldview), while those in particular propositions refer to some (Some men are theists). But what about the predicates? This is where distribution comes in.

Distribution is to terms what quantity is to propositions. A term is said to be distributed when it refers to all the members of its class. Distribution can be designated by a stated or implied *all*. Both the subject and the predicate have distribution, because they are both terms. In the statement, "[W]hoever believes in Him [will] not perish" (John 3:16), the subject is understood to mean "All who believe," which is distributed. But the predicate implies "will be *among* those who will not perish," which is undistributed, because it makes no specific claim to include all who will not perish. (In other words, the statement by itself does not tell us that no one who does not believe will be among those who do not perish.)

Terms have distribution; *propositions* have quantity, which depends on the distribution of the subject. Once we know the distribution of the subject, then we can find the distribution of the predicate. Distribution of each term is always the same for each type (A, E, I, O) of statement. To understand this, we'd better walk through it one type at a time, then look at the overall picture.

Type A—All S is P. Let's use "horses" for the subject and "four-legged animals" for the predicate: "All horses are four-legged animals." The subject is distributed because *all* is stated. What about the predicate? Does it include all four-legged animals? No, it covers only the ones mentioned in the subject (horses). It does not refer to other four-legged animals like cows, dogs, sheep, or goats. So it is undistributed. The proposition might be restated, "All horses are a part of the class `four-legged animals.'" This makes it clear that the predicate does not refer to all the members of its class. And it will always be that way for any Type A statement. The predicate will always include more than the subject, so the subject is always distributed and the predicate is always undistributed.

Type E—No S is P. "No horses are two-legged animals." Again, the subject is distributed, since it clearly applies to all of its members—so this is a universal proposition. Now look at the predicate. Does it refer to all or some two-legged animals? We said that Type A predicates refer only to those included in the subject, but here we are denying that any of the subject is part of the predicate. So what the statement really says is, "None of all the horses in the world are included in all the two-legged animals in the world." Go ahead: make a list of bipeds and see if there are any horses there. You won't find any, but you have to include the *whole* list to reach that conclusion. So both subject and predicate are always distributed in Type E propositions.

Type I—Some S is P. "Some horses are white." At this point we can start looking for principles that carry us through. The subject is undistributed, as it must be in all particular statements. Let's stick with horses (they have carried us this far). The predicate (let's use white) must refer to all white things or some white things. The principle to remember is that in an affirmative statement, what is said applies only to those things specified by the subject. When we affirm that those things included in the subject are also among those things included in the predicate, then the predicate can only be undistributed. The statement is limited to the members of the subject which fall into the wider category of things to which the predicate refers. So Type I propositions always have undistributed subjects and undistributed predicates. The most they can claim is that "Some horses are some of the white things in the world." There are other white things, like pelicans and polar bears, and other horses are not white.

Type O—Some S is not P. You should be catching on now. This is a particular statement, so the subject must be undistributed. Right? Now, what did we say about the predicate last time we looked at a negative statement? It is distributed, isn't it? If you don't understand why, go back and read the paragraph on Type E again. If you deny that something is inside a certain circle, you have to deny that it can be found anywhere in that circle. You have to refer to the whole circle, not just part. Hence, the predicate of Type O propositions is always distributed, and the subject is always undistributed.

Are you ready for the big picture now? *Universal subjects and negative predicates are distributed.* Can you remember that rule? It's not all that hard. By process of elimination, that tells us that affirmative statements always have undistributed predicates, and so do subjects in particular statements. The chart in Figure 2.6. summarizes these relations.

Figure 2.6

	Type	Subject	Copula	Predicate
Universal	A	All S $^{Dist.}$	is	P $^{Undist.}$
	E	All S $^{Dist.}$	is not	P $^{Dist.}$
Particuar	I	Some S $^{Undist.}$	is	P $^{Undist.}$
	O	Some S $^{Undist.}$	is not	P $^{Dist.}$

Notice where terms are marked as distributed: the universal subjects and the negative predicates. Now, since distribution follows so closely along the lines of quality and quantity, another kind of chart may be helpful. In Figure 2.7, the universal types are together on top and the negative types are together on one side, so that we have a square with two axes for quality and quantity. From top to bottom represents quantity (universal and particular, respectively), and from side to side shows quality (right is negative and left is affirmative).

It all boils down to our simple rule: *Universal subjects and negative predicates are distributed.* The rest are not.

Figure 2.7

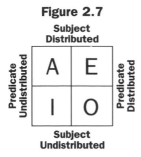

Let's go back over the basics of this chapter one more time before we move on to syllogisms. The smallest building block we have is a term. It takes two of these (subject and predicate) to make a proposition, and they have to be tied together with a copula. The copula may be affirmative or negative, and it determines the quality of the statement. Distribution tells whether a term refers to all or some of the members of its category. Quantifiers may be either stated or implied to help us find the distribution. If the subject of a proposition is distributed, then the statement is universal in quantity; if not, it is particular. The predicates of affirmative propositions are always undistributed, and the predicates of negative propositions are always distributed.

All of that can be simplified to this: There are four types of propositions, A, E, I, and O; universal subjects and negative predicates are always distributed. If you can hang on to that much, you've got it made.

Exercises for Chapter 2

2.1 Identify which of the following are arguments and, if they are, which are deductive and which are inductive.

1. Our university campus study of one hundred students showed a dramatic increase in grades after their becoming Christians; therefore we conclude that conversion to Christianity helps your grade point average.
2. Jesus said, "I am the way, the truth, and the life. No man comes to the Father but through me" (John. 14:6).
3. According to the Bible, all sinners need to trust Christ, and you are a sinner. So you need to trust Christ.

4. "There are no miracles, Jesus was not the Son of God, and there is no God."
5. Robert is a Christian and Christians don't know logic, so it's obvious that Robert doesn't know logic.
6. I know Jesus rose from the dead because he appeared to the disciples, the tomb is empty, and even some of his enemies like Paul came to believe in him.
7. In last night's campus meeting there were thirty-two Catholics, twenty-four nonreligious, and sixteen of various Protestant denominations.
8. The Bible is historically accurate and anything that is historically accurate is trustworthy. So the Bible is trustworthy.
9. Christianity is unique from all the other religions in the world. It is unlike Buddhism, Hinduism and Islam.
10. I know the Bible is trustworthy because of three things: it never contradicts itself, it doesn't contradict other historical writings, and the manuscript evidence is greater than any other writing of ancient times.

2.2 Identify the quantifier (Q), the subject term (S), the copula (C), and the predicate term (P) in the following propositions. Put brackets around each of the four terms.

1. All Christians are saved.
2. No Baptists are Presbyterians.
3. Some people who attend church are not true believers.
4. Salvation is a free gift.
5. Bertrand Russell is an atheist.
6. Some atheists are communists.
7. David Hume wrote an argument against believing in miracles.
8. All communists are atheists.
9. Christians who study their Bibles, pray, and obey Christ, will remain in fellowship with God.
10. No nonbelievers will go to heaven.
11. God does not change.
12. I am not an atheist.
13. All people are descendants of Adam.
14. Some descendants of Adam are believers in Christ.
15. Some people are not believers in Christ.

2.3 Identify the following propositions as either universal or particular and as affirmative or negative.

1. Some people are non-Christians. *PA*
2. No atheists are Christians. *UN*
3. Some Hindus are not pantheists. *PN*
4. Sharon is a member of First Baptist Church. *UA*
5. All believers are going to heaven. *UA*
6. Logic is not used by everybody. *UN*
7. Some angels fell with Satan. *PA*
8. God cannot sin. *UA*
9. Unhappy people are people who need the Lord. *PA/UA*
10. None is righteous. *UN*
11. Some Christians are not obedient people. *PN*
12. Some Christians are non-obedient people. *PA*
13. No man has seen God. *UN*
14. All men are not saved.
15. All nonbelievers are non-Christians.
16. Many unsaved people are good neighbors.

2.4 Identify the following as either A, E, I, or O propositions.

1. No disciples are unkind. *E*
2. Paul was a champion of Christianity. *A*
3. Some church attenders are not paying attention. *O*
4. All Scripture is inspired. (2 Tim. 3:16) *A*
5. Some theologians are wrong. *I*
6. Each and every person needs to trust Christ for his salvation. *A*
7. Nobody seeks God. (Rom. 3:10) *E*
8. God is immutable. *A*
9. They are not among the believers. *O E*
10. Those books are in the Bible. *A A*
11. Not all preachers are Protestant. *O*

2.5 Determine the type of the following propositions (A, E, I, or O) and the distribution of both the subject and predicate terms.

1. All enemies of Christ will be defeated.
2. No nonbelievers can understand the things of the Spirit.

3. The Apostle John is the disciple whom Jesus loved.
4. The Bible is the Word of God.
5. Some roads lead to destruction.
6. Some who are standing here will see the kingdom of God.
7. Most atheists are immoral.
8. All unhappy people are not nonbelievers.
9. Judy is not being a good witness for Christ.
10. Some Christians are not nonsmokers.
11. These arguments are ineffective for Christianity.
12. Christ is impeccable.
13. Some who obey Christ are not unfulfilled.
14. No non-Christians will see heaven.
15. Immoral persons can't be trusted.

2.6 For Advanced Students: Here are some challenging exercises. Identify the type and distribution of the following propositions.

1. Nothing ventured, nothing gained.
2. God loves you.
3. Some person is not going to heaven.
4. All atheists are not cruel.
5. Not to trust Christ is to disobey Scripture.
6. All who are not guilty are innocent.
7. Something is better than nothing.
8. None but believers will go to heaven.
9. Everyone except George became a Christian at last night's meeting.
10. Only Jesus can answer the world's problems.

3

Basic Logical Structures

Now that we know what logic is all about and what the building blocks for logical thought are, it's time to start doing some real deduction. The basic tool of all deductive logic is the syllogism (pronounced *sil-o-jism*.) It is easy to recognize. Whenever you see two propositions that have one term in common and are followed by a conclusion (a proposition that might be introduced by *hence, therefore, so,* or *thus*), that's a syllogism. It may not be a good one, but it is a syllogism. Simply speaking, a syllogism is the format that we use to put the propositions together so that we can analyze their relationships to one another to see if they make sense. Having said that, let's see if we can put one together and make it fly.

Parts of a Syllogism

The most basic kind of syllogism is called a *categorical syllogism.* It is called *categorical* because it is made up of two unconditional premises leading to an unconditional conclusion: in other words, three categorical statements.

The relationships between these statements are very important. The statements have a lot in common. In fact, there can be no more than three terms to fill all six subject and predicate slots. The first term is the *major term.* It occurs in the major premise and is the *predicate* of the conclusion. The second term is the *minor term,* which is found in the minor premise and is the *subject* of the conclusion. The third term is shared by both premises but never appears in the conclusion; it is the *middle term*. The terms might fill the subject and predicate slots like this:

	Figure 1	Figure 2	Figure 3	Figure 4
Premise 1	Middle/Major	Major/Middle	Middle/Major	Major/Middle
Premise 2	Minor/Middle or	Minor/Middle or	Middle/Minor or	Middle/Minor
Conclusion	Minor/Major	Minor/Major	Minor/Major	Minor/Major

We will talk about how the middle term moves around later, but for now it is important just to know that the minor and major terms are *always* the subject and predicate of the conclusion, respectively, and the middle term is common to both premises, but is never in the conclusion.

Here is an example:

Major premise: All lost persons *(middle term)* are unbelievers *(major term)*.

Minor premise: All sinners *(minor term)* are lost persons *(middle term)*.

Conclusion: All sinners *(minor term)* are unbelievers *(major term)*.

That's not too hard, is it?

Seven Rules of the Categorical Syllogism

There are seven simple rules for how to make a valid syllogism. Remember, *validity* doesn't guarantee *truth;* the truth of the premises and their relevance to the subject also must be examined. But these rules will tell us how to put good premises together in a good format to make a good argument.

1. *There must be only three terms.* Sometimes an ambiguous fourth (or more) term sneaks into a syllogism by means of an *equivocation* (when a term has one meaning the first time it appears but a different meaning the next time it is used) or by *slipping the middle term into the conclusion.*

Here is an example of adding a fourth term by using an equivocal middle term:

All inspired writings are included in the Scriptures.
Handel was inspired when he wrote the *Messiah.*
Therefore, Handel's *Messiah* should be included in the Scriptures.

This sounds good at first. But the problem is that *inspired* in the first premise does not mean the same as *inspired* in the second premise. In the first premise, the term means that the writing was directed by God, or "God-breathed," but in the second premise, it means that a man was simply in an exhilarated state. That means that there are actually four terms used in this argument (God-breathed, Scriptures, exhilarated, and *Messiah*), and that's tabu.

Here is an example of slipping the middle term into the conclusion:

All the books of the Bible are inerrant.
Some of the books of the Bible were written by Paul.
Therefore, some of the books of the Bible are inerrant.

Notice that all of the propositions are true. However, there is no inference from the first and second premise to the conclusion. You can reach this conclusion on the basis of the first premise alone. Since in logic our goal is to reach an inference from two propositions, slipping the middle term into the conclusion is also tabu.

2. *The middle term must be distributed at least once.* A term is distributed when it applies to all members of its class (an implied *all* or *none*). Why is it so important that the middle term be distributed? Well, if it does not speak about all in the class, then it might leave something out—maybe even the group that we want to talk about in the syllogism. Such a mistake is sometimes called the fallacy of "Undistributed Middle." Remember that the middle term is shared by both premises, so the conclusion tells us how those two premises relate to each other *with respect to the middle term.* If it doesn't refer to all of its category at least once, there might not be any relation at all between the two premises. Look at this example (the raised *D*'s and *U*'s indicate whether a term is distributed or undistributed):

All Baptists^D are baptized^U.
All Presbyterians^D are baptized^U.
Therefore, all Presbyterians^D are Baptists^U.

Somehow that just doesn't sound right. The middle term (in this case, *baptized*) needs to refer to the *whole* of some group before we can conclude that the sub-groups are included. When in doubt, draw some circles, like those in Figure 3.1.

Figure 3.1

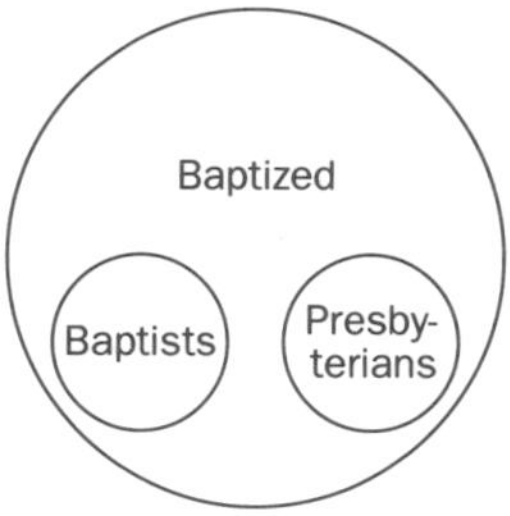

3. *Terms distributed in the conclusion must be distributed in the premises.* If we try to make a term refer to all of its class in the conclusion when it referred only to a part in the premises, then we are putting more in the conclusion than we had to begin with. You can't put half a gallon of water in the jug and expect to pour a whole gallon out. Some call it the fallacy of "Illicit Process." The conclusion must never talk about more of the group than does the premise. It might refer to less, because there is no rule saying that a distributed term can't be undistributed in the conclusion. Often that is the case. But it must never refer to more. For example:

All Hindus are vegetarians (a *part* of the vegetarian community).
No Jehovah's Witness is a Hindu.
Therefore, no Jehovah's Witness is a vegetarian (the *whole* vegetarian community).

As you can see, the result is an equivocation similar to the four-term fallacy of rule 1.

4. *The conclusion always follows the weaker premise.* If the size of the group can't increase in the conclusion (rule 3), neither can the strength of the assertion. If one of the premises is particular (some), the conclusion must be particular. If one of the premises is negative, the conclusion must be negative. The chain of an argument is no stronger than its weakest link. This can be a very helpful rule, because it tells us the quantity and quality of the conclusion before we get there. Try this one:

No wicked person will escape judgment. (universal/negative)
Some Americans are wicked. (particular/affirmative)

Because the major premise is negative, the conclusion must be negative. Because the minor premise is particular, the conclusion cannot be universal. Hence, the conclusion must be a Type O statement (particular/negative):

Therefore, some Americans will not escape judgment.

5. *No conclusion follows from two negative premises.* This one is not hard to figure out. If nothing from one group has anything in common with anything from another group, there is nothing you can say about the two groups in common. As Richard Rogers' popular song said, "Nothing comes from nothing: nothing ever could." This is often called the fallacy of "Exclusive Premises" because the two negative premises exclude the possibility of any relation between them.

No humans are angels.
No angels are God.
Therefore, ? .

6. *No conclusion follows from two simple particular premises.*[1] A simple particular is one where *some* means not more than half. This would mean that your conclusion refers to less than half of less than half of the minor premise. But you can't say for sure that some fit the conclusion when it is very likely that none fit. Sure, there might be some cases where it works out to be true, but a syllogism based on the possibility is not valid because there is no case where the conclusion follows necessarily. And deductive logic, remember, deals with necessary conclusions. One might argue,

Some premillennialists are charismatic.
Some Catholics are charismatic.
Therefore, some Catholics are premillennialists.

---

1. Many omit this rule, since it cannot be broken without already breaking one of the other rules of distribution.

It is possible that that's true, but few Catholics would be willing to reject centuries of their church's teaching in favor of amillennialism. Let's put it this way: If you invited all Catholic premillennialists to a prayer and fellowship meeting, you might wind up eating all the donuts yourself.

7. *No negative conclusion follows from two affirmative premises.* Jesus said, "Let your statement be `Yes, yes' or `No, no'." Well, the same principle applies to logic. You can't say "Yes, yes" in the premises and "No" in the conclusion. In rule 5, we said that nothing comes from nothing. Here we are turning that around to say, "From something must come something." Also, rule 4 said that the conclusion follows the weaker premise, but if both premises are positive, then the weakest possible conclusion is still positive. There is just no way to sneak a negative into the conclusion if it wasn't there in the premises.

Some people have tried to reason this way:

All members of the Trinity are fully God.
Some members of the Trinity take orders from God the Father (e.g., the Son and Spirit are sent, John 16:5–7)
Therefore, not all members of the Trinity are equal to God the Father.

This argument has been used for ages to show that Christ was not equal with God, but obviously the conclusion does not follow. No negative conclusion can come from affirmative premises. So the conclusion should be, "Some who take orders from the Father are fully God." They are still God, but act in voluntary submission.

That's all! Those are the seven rules for evaluating all syllogisms. We hope learning them wasn't too painful. Having mastered these rules, let's talk about the different forms a syllogism can have.

Forms: Figures and Moods of the Categorical Syllogism

Two factors combine to make up the form of a syllogism: figure and mood. *Figure* refers to *the position of the middle term in the premises. Mood* refers to *the relationship of the quality and quantity of the two premises* (A–E–I–O). Using the rules we just learned, we can evaluate any syllogism by its figure and mood to see if it is valid. So if you're in the mood, let's figure it out.

Figures

The figure is the positions the middle term takes in the premises. Assuming standard syllogism form (major premise first, minor second), there are four possible figures, named first, second, third, and fourth (it took a real genius to think of that one). Figure 3.2 shows the four possible positions that the middle term can have: (M = middle term, P = predicate [major term], and S = subject [minor term]). The middle term will always be either first in the first premise and second in the second, or second in both, or first in both, or second in the first and first in the second.

Figure 3.2

	Figure 1	Figure 2	Figure 3	Figure 4
Major Premise	M P	P M	M P	P M
Minor Premise	S M	S M	M S	M S

"Why in the world does it matter where the middle term is?" you might ask. Think back: we said earlier that syllogistic reasoning depends entirely on (a) the relationship between the major and minor terms, and (b) in respect to what they have in common with the middle term. *The figure tells us what the relation of the middle term is to each of the other terms.* That relationship is not interchangeable. You know that ten minus two is not the same as two minus ten. The same idea applies in logic. "All horses are four-legged creatures" does not mean the same as "All four-legged creatures are horses" (horses are only some of the four-legged creatures). By the same token, "God is love" does not mean the same as "Love is God" (love is only part of what God is). So knowing where the middle term occurs is important. Figures can tell us that.

Any term that occurs twice in a syllogism must be important to the argument. We said earlier that the middle term must be distributed at least once. The figure will determine whether the predicate is a *subset* of the subject, the *set* of which the subject is a part, if they are both the *same set*, or if they are *overlapping sets.* It all depends on what the relation of the middle term is to the major and minor terms; in other words, figure. In fact, we are about to see that some syllogisms are valid only in certain figures. But for that, we have to understand mood.

Moods

Mood is determined by the relationship between the premises in regard to their quality and quantity (types A, E, I, and O). There are sixty-four possible moods, as laid out in Figure 3.3, but only eleven of these moods are valid, and most only in certain figures. Why? Because of The Seven Rules of the Syllogism! The chart is to be read vertically, with the top two characters representing types of statements (A, E, I, and O) used in the premises of a syllogism, and the last, its conclusion. Each of eleven valid moods is marked with a box. The three broken-lined boxes mark moods that are valid only for weak conclusions in some figures. These exhaust the logical possibilities for the mood of a syllogism.

Figure 3.3
Possible Mood Chart

Major	A	A	A	A	E	E	E	E	I	I	I	I	O	O	O	O
Minor	A	E	I	O	A	E	I	O	A	E	I	O	A	E	I	O
Conclusion	A	A	A	A	A	A	A	A	A	A	A	A	A	A	A	A

Major	A	A	A	A	E	E	E	E	I	I	I	I	O	O	O	O
Minor	A	E	I	O	A	E	I	O	A	E	I	O	A	E	I	O
Conclusion	E	E	E	E	E	E	E	E	E	E	E	E	E	E	E	E

Major	A	A	A	A	E	E	E	E	I	I	I	I	O	O	O	O
Minor	A	E	I	O	A	E	I	O	A	E	I	O	A	E	I	O
Conclusion	I	I	I	I	I	I	I	I	I	I	I	I	I	I	I	I

Major	A	A	A	A	E	E	E	E	I	I	I	I	O	O	O	O
Minor	A	E	I	O	A	E	I	O	A	E	I	O	A	E	I	O
Conclusion	O	O	O	O	O	O	O	O	O	O	O	O	O	O	O	O

As you can see from the chart, some moods cannot possibly be valid. For example, the first column lists the possibilities for AA premises (both affirmative and universal). But it is not possible to have a negative conclusion from positive premises (Remember rule 7?), so the conclusions E and O are clearly not valid. In fact, large portions of the chart are done away with by this rule, and more are eliminated by rule 5, disallowing conclusions from negative premises. By the time we apply all the rules to the chart, we are left with only eight moods that are valid and yield strong conclusions: AAA, AEE, AII, AOO, EAE, EIO, IAI, and OAO. Three other moods (AAI, EAO, and AEO) yield weaker conclusions when a strong conclusion is possible. For instance, AA premises can yield an A conclusion (strong), but AAI is valid also; if all fit the category, then some do, too. The same is true of moods AEO and EAO as well. Their conclusions are weaker, but the forms are still valid. Figure 3.4 shows which moods are valid in each figure.

Figure 3.4
Figures and Valid Moods

Figure 1	Figure 2	Figure 3	Figure 4
M P	P M	M P	P M
\	|	|	/
S M	S M	M S	M S

AAA	EAE	AAI	AAI
EAE	AEE	EAO	AEE
AII	EIO	IAI	IAI
EIO	AOO	AII	EAO
(AAI)	(AEO)	OAO	EIO
(EAO)	(EAO)	EIO	AEO

(Moods in parentheses yield only weak conclusions.)

This chart gives us a ready reference for evaluating all syllogisms. *If the format of the argument does not correspond to one of the moods on the chart in the figure under which it is listed, it can't be valid.*

Beyond this, the chart teaches us several things about the importance of the figure.

1. No O premise occurs in the first figure.
2. Universal affirmative conclusions (Type A) occur only in the first figure.
3. There must be one and only one negative premise (E or O) in the second figure.
4. All conclusions in the second figure are negative (E or O).
5. All conclusions of the third figure are particular (I or O).

The chart also provides a summary of the figures available in each of the valid moods (Moods in parentheses yield only weak conclusions.):

Mood	Figure 1	Figure 2	Figure 3	Figure 4
AAA	OK	Undistributed Middle	Illicit Minor	Illicit Minor
(AAI)	OK (Weak)	Undistributed Middle	OK	OK
AEE	Illicit Major	OK	Illicit Major	Ok
(AEO)	Illicit Major	OK (Weak)	Illicit Major	OK
AII	OK	Undistributed Middle	OK	Undistributed Middle
AOO	Illicit Major	OK	Illicit Major	Undistributed Middle
EAE	OK	OK	Illicit Minor	Illicit Minor
(EAO)	OK (Weak)	OK (Weak)	OK	OK
EIO	OK	OK	OK	OK
IAI	Undistributed Middle	Undistributed Middle	OK	OK
OAO	Undistributed Middle	Illicit Major	OK	Illicit Major

Chart by Kenneth L. Hood

Because syllogistic reasoning relies on these forms, any argument that takes an invalid form can be refuted. If someone tries to build an argument on an invalid form, you could respond by saying, "That's just like arguing—" and giving an example of a syllogism in the same form that is clearly false. If the form is invalid, the argument cannot stand.

Fallacies of the Categorical Syllogism

What if the mood and figure check out, but there is still something that doesn't sound right? That is where the fallacies can help us. Mood and figure are governed by rules 4 through 7 of the syllogism. The fallacies are covered in rules 1 through 3. Let's review these now; examples can be found in chapter 5.

1. **Illicit Major**—The major term is distributed in the conclusion but not in the premise.
2. **Illicit Minor**—The minor term is distributed in the conclusion but not in the premise.
3. **Undistributed Middle**—The middle term is not distributed at least once.
4. **Four-Term Fallacy**—There are not three and only three terms in the argument (includes "ambiguous middle" and "equivocal middle" fallacies).

As you can see, the illicit major and minor are derived from rule 3. (Because of this, both are sometimes called *Illicit Process*, distinguished as *Illicit Process of the Major Term* and *Illicit Process of the Minor Term*.) Undistributed middle restates rule 2, and the four-term fallacy comes from rule 1. So we are right back where we began with the seven rules of the syllogism providing all we need to evaluate categorical syllogisms.

Immediate Deductions and the Square of Opposition

Before moving on to other types of syllogisms, something needs to be said about the different ways to change a proposition. Any categorical proposition implies some other categorical propositions. Obviously, if "All are," then "None are not." And if "Some do," then it is not true that "None do." There are two kinds of operations to discuss here. A proposition can be changed into a different type of statement with the same meaning (immediate deductions), or a different type of statement can be constructed from the same terms (relations among propositions).

An *immediate deduction* is a deduction that can be drawn directly from a statement without knowing anything else. For example:

Original statement: All men are sinful.
Immediate deduction: No men are non-sinful.

Unlike a syllogism that involves a *mediate* deduction of one proposition from another (by way of a third proposition), an *immediate* deduction can be drawn directly from one proposition to another. There are three such operations possible: Obversion, Conversion, and Contraposition.

1. *Obversion*: In obversion we *change the quality (affirmative or negative) of a statement without changing its meaning.* Here we change "is" (or "are") to "is not" (or "are not").

A obverts to E: "All men are fallible" becomes
                "No men are infallible."
E obverts to A: "No men are infallible" becomes
                "All men are non-infallible" (= "All men are
                fallible").

I obverts to O: "Some men are pastors" becomes
                  "Some men are not non-pastors."
O obverts to I: "Some men are not teachers" becomes
                  "Some men are non-teachers."

2. *Conversion:* In conversion we *change the relation (or order) of subject and predicate without changing its meaning.*

A does not convert.[2]
E converts to E: "No demons are good" becomes
                   "No good (beings) are demons."
I converts to I: "Some angels have appeared as humans"
                   becomes
                   "Some who appeared to be human were
                   angels."
O does not convert to anything.

3. *Contraposition:* In contraposition, we *obvert a converted obverse of the original proposition.* For example:

A original: All born again are saved.
E obverse: No born again are unsaved.
E converse: No unsaved are born again.
A obverse: All unsaved are non-born again (the contrapositive of the first sentence).

A contraposes to A
E does not contrapose.
I does not contrapose
O contraposes to O

Now, before you go crazy trying to figure out that last one, let's back up and discuss this whole thing. Obversion is pretty simple. You change the quality of the statement (affirmative to negative or vice-versa) *and* you negate the predicate term. Conversion gets

---

2. Since the predicate of a Type A is undistributed, it can only convert by limitation to a Type I: "All horses (distributed) are in the category of four-legged animals" (undistributed) converts only to "Some four-legged animals (undistributed) are in the category of horses" (undistributed). In short, you can go from all to some but not from some to all.

a little stickier, because when you switch the subject and the predicate around, all the *all*s and some of the *some*s have to change too. The Type O statement won't convert for that very reason. The true statement, "Some created beings are not humans," would yield the false converse, "Some humans are not created beings."

When we form a contrapositive, we are changing the order of subject and predicate (conversion) and changing the quality of the statement *twice*. Since two negatives make a positive (just like in multiplication), the quality of the statement will remain the same. But the quantity of the statement may need to change in the conversion process. This is the case for the E proposition, as we see if we follow it through the process. It would first obvert to an A proposition, but the A converts to an I, changing the *all* to *some*. The second obversion returns to the negative value and we have an O contrapositive. The reason that the I statement has no contrapositive becomes clear if we use the same method. It would first obvert to an O statement. *Now what is the problem with the next step?* (Here's a hint: how does an O statement convert?) Now you're catching on! You can't have a contrapositive if you can't complete the process.

Obversion, conversion, and contraposition are the only valid deductions we can make immediately from any given statement by itself. We can use them to clarify an argument stated in an unclear way, to change the mood of a syllogism, or to expose a fault in someone's reasoning when he attempts to use an invalid restatement. But what relations can be found between *different* statements that have the same terms? There are seven relations that can be seen. The first two are relations of compatibility, and the remaining five are relations of opposition.

1. *Independence. The truth or falsity of one statement has no bearing on the truth or falsity of the other.* There is simply no connection between the two statements, so if the truth of one statement is known, the truth or falsity of the other cannot be determined immediately (The symbol ∴ means *therefore*.):

P true ∴ Q? (undetermined) P: Jesus rose from the dead.
P false ∴ Q? (undetermined) Q: I had a spiritual experience.

These two statements have no relation to each other.

2. *Equivalence. Equivalent propositions will always be true or false together.* This is the case with all immediate propositions:

P true ∴ Q true   P: All of God is everywhere.
P false ∴ Q false   Q: None of God is nowhere.

What immediate deduction explains the relation between these statements?

The next five relations are summarized in the Square of Opposition below. (See Figure 3.5.)

3. *Contradiction. The truth of one necessarily involves the falsity of the other and vice versa.* Both cannot be true; both cannot be false. This occurs in two statements of the same terms but opposed in *both* quality and quantity. Statements of types A and O can contradict each other, as can statements of types E and I.

P true ∴ Q false   P: All truth is relative.
P false ∴ Q true   Q: Some truths are not relative.

The first statement would negate the second if it were true. However, P here is put forth as an absolute truth, implying that Q is true. Therefore, P must be false.

4. *Contrariety. The truth of one involves the falsity of the other, but the falsity of one does not necessarily involve the truth of the other.* They cannot both be true, but they could both be false. This occurs when universal statements differ in quality, but not in quantity. Contrariety occurs only between Type A and Type E statements.

P true ∴ Q false   P: All men will be judged.
P false ∴ Q? (undetermined) Q: No men will be judged.

If the first statement is true, the second must be false. But if not all men are judged it is still possible that some will be, so we cannot tell about the truth of the second statement.

5. *Subcontrariety. The truth of one does not necessarily involve the falsity of the other, but the falsity of one does involve the truth of the other.* Both can be true, but only one can be false. This is like contrariety but applies to particular propositions, rather than universals. Subcontrariety occurs only between statements of Type I and Type O.

P true ∴ Q? (undetermined)   P: Some people are Billy
    Graham.
P false ∴ Q true   Q: Some people are not Billy Graham.

Both of these can be true, but if either one is false, the other
has to be true.

6. *Subalternation. The truth of one involves the truth of the other,
but the falsity of one does not necessarily involve the falsity of the other.*
While both statements can be true, the falsity of one leaves the
other undetermined. This occurs when a universal premise is
compared to a particular premise of the same quality. Subalternation is a one-way relation from statements of Type A to Type I
and from statements of Type E to Type O.

P true ∴ Q true   P: All Christians are sincere.
P false ∴ Q? (undetermined) Q: Some Christians are sincere.

If the universal statement is false, it is still possible that the
particular statement is true, but we don't know. However, if it is
true for all, then it is true for some.

7. *Superalternation. The truth of one does not necessarily involve the
truth of the other, but the falsity of one does involve the falsity of the
other.* Here both might be true (that cannot be determined), but
if one is false, both must be false. This occurs when a particular
premise is related to its corresponding universal of the same
quality. Superalternation is a one-way relation from statements
of Type I to Type A and from statements of Type O to Type E.

P true ∴ Q? (undetermined) P: Some theistic proofs are not
                              logical.
P false ∴ Q false   Q: No theistic proofs are logical.

While the truth of the first still allows that some other proofs
might be logical, the truth of the universal statement remains
undetermined. On the other hand, if the particular statement is
false (i.e., if all proofs turn out to be logical), then it cannot be
true that no theistic proofs are logical.

These relations can be seen more clearly in Figure 3.5, which
shows the Square of Opposition. The universal propositions are
on the top corners, and the particulars are on the bottom cor-

Figure 3.5
Square of Opposition

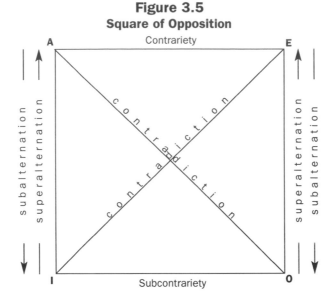

ners. The right side is negative, and the left affirmative. The name of the relation between any two given corners is stated on the line between those corners. Study this chart with the explanations given above, and see why each of the conclusions follows in the summary of relations given below in Figure 3.6.

The square of opposition comes in handy because we can use it to discover the truth value of other corresponding propositions.

Figure 3.6
Table of Valid Inferences

	A is	E is	I is	O is
If A is true		False	True	False
If A is false		Undetermined	Undetermined	True
If E is true	False		False	True
If E is false	Undetermined		True	Undetermined
If I is true	Undetermined	False		Undetermined
If I is false	False	True		True
If O is true	False	Undetermined	Undetermined	
If O is false	True	False	True	

This helps us to see immediately whether the other propositions are true or false in relation to the one with which we begin.

Exercises for Chapter 3

3.1 Identify the major (M), minor (m), and middle (mid) terms and major (M) and minor (m) premises in the following syllogisms.

1. All agnostics deny any knowledge of God.
   Those who deny any knowledge of God do not make sense.
   Agnostics do not make sense.

2. Some people attend church.
   All Christians attend church.
   Some people are Christians.

3. Everything that has a beginning must have had a cause.
   The universe had a beginning.
   The universe must have had a cause.

4. Some atheists are not moral.
   Renee is an atheist.
   Renee is not moral.

5. No books of the Bible are in error.
   Some books of the Bible are books written by Paul.
   All books written by Paul are not in error.

6. All men are sinners.
   I am a man.
   I am a sinner.

7. All S is M.
   No M is P.
   No S is P.

8. The Bible is the Word of God.
   The Word of God cannot err.
   The Bible cannot err.

9. All who have faith in Jesus are saved.
   Sharon does not have faith in Jesus.
   Sharon is not saved.

10. Those who obey Christ are believers.
    Some Christians do not obey Christ.
    Some Christians are not believers.

3.2 Using the rules we learned in this chapter, discover the validity or invalidity of the following syllogisms. If any are invalid, name the rule being broken. When you have finished these, go back and do the same with the exercises in 3.1. *Remember: The validity of an argument does not make it true and truthfulness does not make an argument valid.* Don't be fooled!

1. No Christians are unsaved.
   Some people are unsaved.
   Some people are not Christians.

2. Every a is b.
   Every b is c.
   Every c is a.

3. Nothing is better than heaven.
   Life on earth is better than nothing.
   Life on earth is better than heaven.

4. No a is b.
   No b is c.
   No c is a.

5. All men are substances.
   All who are saved are substances.
   All who are saved are men.

6. No P is Q.
   Some S is P.
   Some S is not Q.

7. Some believers are Americans.
   Some church attenders are not Americans.
   Some believers are church attenders.

8. All Bible manuscripts have errors.
   Some errors are certain.
   No manuscripts are certain.

9. All that exists is matter.
   God is not matter.
   God does not exist.

10. A moral absolute is necessary.
    God is necessary.
    God is the moral absolute.

11. Miracles do not exist.
    Miracles prove the existence of God.
    Proof of the existence of God does not exist.

12. Evil is not a substance.
    All substances are created by God.
    Evil is not created by God.

13. Jesus Christ is not a sinner.
    Jesus Christ rose from the dead. 4T
    Jesus Christ is God.
14. No unbelievers are heaven-bound.
    Some who are heaven-bound are not church attenders.
    Some unbelievers are not church attenders.   EP
15. What can be perceived with our senses is true.
    The existence of the soul is not perceived with our
    senses.
    The existence of the soul is not true. I M

3.3 Return to the exercises in 3.1. and 3.2. Identify the figure of the middle term for each syllogism. Remember that the figure depends on placing the major premise first.

3.4 Again using the exercises in 3.1 and 3.2, name the mood for each syllogism. Be sure to list the types of statements in the order of major premise, minor premise, conclusion.

3.5 Equivalent sentences

a. Obvert the following propositions:
    1. All believers are saved.
    2. Some arguments for God are not valid.
    3. Jesus Christ is God.
    4. No person is righteous.
    5. Some atheists are immoral.
    6. Morality is universally recognized.
    7. All nonbelievers are unsaved.
    8. No book of the Bible is uninspired.
    9. Some philosophers are not non-Christians.
    10. God is a necessary being.
b. Convert the following propositions:
    1. Some angels are fallen.
    2. No theologians are infallible.
    3. All the books in the Bible are inerrant.
    4. Tom is not a believer.
    5. Some deists are not British.
    6. Some people are unsaved.
    7. Tom is a nonbeliever.
c. Contrapose the following propositions:

1. All religions are unequal.
2. Some nonbelievers are not unkind.
3. No Christians are nonbelievers.
4. Some beliefs are not unwarranted.
5. The Bible is invaluable.
6. Some logical statements are almost impossible to understand.
7. All non-atheists are believers.
8. No book of the Bible is incorrect.
9. Nonhumans are unintelligent.
10. Some propositions are not contraposable.

3.6 Using the Square of Opposition, along with the relationships of independence and equivalence, determine the truth value (i.e., true, false, or undetermined) of the propositions that follow the original.

1. "All atheists are enemies of Christ." is true:
   a. No atheists are enemies of Christ.
   b. Some atheists are enemies of Christ.
   c. Some atheists are not enemies of Christ.
2. "No people are seeking God." is true:
   a. Some people are seeking God.
   b. All people are seeking God.
   c. No seekers after God are people.
3. "Some humans are nonbelievers." is false:
   a. No humans are nonbelievers.
   b. All believers are people.
   c. Some humans are not nonbelievers.
4. "No books of the Bible are inerrant." is false:
   a. All books of the Bible are inerrant.
   b. Some books of the Bible are not inerrant.
   c. All books of the Bible are errant.
5. "Some atheists are not immoral." is true:
   a. Some immoral persons are not atheists.
   b. No atheists are immoral.
   c. All atheists are not immoral.
6. "All biblical manuscripts are erroneous." is true:
   a. No nonbiblical manuscripts are erroneous.
   b. All non-erroneous things are biblical manuscripts.
   c. No non-erroneous things are nonbiblical manuscripts.

7. "Some P is not Q." is false:
   a. All P is Q.
   b. No P is Q.
   c. Some P is Q.
8. "No religion is completely wrong." is true:
   a. Some religions are completely wrong.
   b. No completely wrong things are religions.
   c. All religions are completely wrong.
9. "All created things are contingent." is true:
   a. No created things are contingent.
   b. Some created things are contingent.
   c. Some created things are not contingent.
10. "All created things are contingent." is false:
    a. No created things are contingent.
    b. Some created things are contingent.
    c. Some created things are not contingent.

3.7 For Advanced Students: Using all that we have learned in this chapter, determine the validity or invalidity of the following arguments. If any are invalid explain why. You may have to change (obvert, convert, contrapose) some of the premises before determining validity. These are tricky, so think hard.

1. Julie loves Jesus.
   Paul loves Julie.
   Paul loves Jesus.
2. All atheists are nonbelievers.
   All believers are going to heaven.
   No atheists are going to heaven.
3. Since some Christians are good debaters, it follows that some Christians are not good debaters.
4. All who are not guilty are innocent.
   Some are not guilty.
   Some are innocent.
5. All religious persons are moral persons.
   All immoral persons are scoundrels.
   No religious persons are scoundrels. м   4
6. Not to obey the Bible is to disobey God.
   Not to evangelize is not to obey the Bible.
   Not to evangelize is to disobey God.

7. Since no religious person is completely in the dark, it is false that some religious persons are completely in the dark.

8. Only people are savable.
   Some living things are savable.
   All people are living things.

9. No P are M.
   All S are M.
   Some S are not P.

10. All explosives are flammable.
    All inflammable things are unsafe.
    All safe things are nonexplosives.

[handwritten notes:] All non flammable things are nonexplosive
All unsafe things as nonflammable
All

4

Other Types of Syllogisms

There you are cringing with terror, screaming, "No! No! Not more syllogisms! Anything but that!" Relax; these are the easy ones. They're more familiar because they probably are seen more frequently than categorical syllogisms, and the rules for them are much simpler. We call them compound syllogisms because they are composed of different kinds of sentences as their premises (i.e., not all are categorical propositions as before). All we have to do in this chapter is discuss the kinds of compound syllogisms and mention one other kind of syllogism that doesn't fit anywhere else. Just a handful of formats to learn! How tough can it be?

Since this chapter is going to be so easy, we'll throw in something new along the way. It is called *symbolic logic*. All that means is that we can use symbols instead of words for the basic, common operations in logic. For example, in a categorical syllogism we are constantly repeating "is" or "is not" in every sentence. Instead of writing that out every time, we can use the symbol < for "is" and ≮ for "is not." For the ever-present "Therefore," we use the symbol ∴ . That way we can use a shorthand to check the validity of the argument, like this:

	Translation:	
S < P		All S is P
P ≮ X		No P is X
∴ S ≮ X		Therefore, no S is X.

See how easy that is? You might go back and try out these symbols on some of the syllogisms in Chapter 3. As we come to new terms, we will introduce the symbols as well, and you can use them as you work your way through the book.

Hypothetical Syllogisms

The first kind of compound syllogism we need to discuss is the hypothetical syllogism. Actually, the syllogism as a whole is not hypothetical, but one of its premises is. It is built around an "If . . . then" statement. But if we used three "if P, then Q" statements, we would have a pretty iffy conclusion. This kind of syllogism must be constructed of a conditional major premise and an unconditional minor premise leading to an unconditional conclusion.

Rather than three terms (the number in categorical syllogisms), hypothetical syllogisms have only two. Instead of talking about subjects and predicates, here we have antecedents and consequents. The antecedent is the "If" part of the statement. It states the condition under which the "then" part is true. The consequent is the "then" part—the consequence of (or what follows from) the antecedent if the "If" part is true. All the minor premise has to do is say that the "If" part "is" or the "then" part "is not." Either way, we get a valid conclusion.

Modus Ponens: *Affirming the Antecedent*

The first way to get a valid conclusion from a hypothetical (conditional) premise is to affirm the antecedent. This is called *modus ponens*, from the Latin meaning "way of affirmation." That is, the minor premise will say that the "If" is not just a speculation but a reality. Now, if the "If" is true, then the "then" has to follow, and that becomes our conclusion. We use a sideways horseshoe to indicate "If ⊃ then" relations.

If P, then Q.	(P ⊃ Q)
P	(P)
Therefore, Q	(∴ Q)

If you can put an argument into symbolic logic that looks like this, then you have a *modus ponens* argument. By George, that very sentence you just read is a conditional major premise! So now if we add to it a sentence that says, "This argument can be put into symbolic logic that looks like that," then we can conclude, "Therefore, we have just discovered our first modus ponens argument!"

This type of argument is quite common and very clear, as long as the relationship between antecedent and consequent is not questionable. For example, one of the basic arguments for Christ's deity is this:

If Jesus Christ rose from the dead, then he is God's Son.
Jesus Christ rose from the dead.
Therefore, he is God's Son.

The major premise asserts the connection between Christ's resurrection (the antecedent) and his deity (the consequent). If this connection is real, then it remains only to affirm that he rose; after that the consequent is the only proper conclusion.

Arguments for the existence of God also affirm the antecedent. One form of the cosmological argument can be stated as follows:

If a contingent being exists, then a necessary being must exist as its cause.
A contingent being exists.
Therefore, a necessary being must exist as its cause.

Every contingent (dependent) being is, by definition, dependent on something else for its existence. The major premise spells out the implication that any dependent being must have a necessary cause. The minor premise asserts that the antecedent is real. I, for example, am dependent, not necessary. So, the conclusion follows: there must be a necessary cause somewhere for my existence.

The argument from design uses the same type of reasoning.

If there is design in the universe, then there must have been a Designer.
There is design in the universe.
Therefore, there must have been a Designer.

You can't get any more straightforward than that. This argument fits the model of *modus ponens* to a tee.

$d \supset D$
d
$\therefore D$

Modus Tollens: *Denying the Consequent*

The other valid form for a hypothetical syllogism is to deny that the consequent is true. Want to guess what the Latin meaning is? Right—"the way of denial." If there is a real connection between the antecedent and the consequent (the "If" and the "then"), and the consequent is false, then the antecedent must be false also. If the antecedent were true, then the consequent would not be false (that's what *modus ponens* said). Here are the symbols for this form:

If P, then Q	$P \supset Q$
Not Q	$\sim Q$
Therefore, Not P	$\therefore \sim P$

Notice the new symbol here? It is a negation sign ($\sim$), not a squiggle. We use it whenever we want to deny a term or proposition; that is, when we want to say that something is false. We use it here to deny the consequent, which leads us to the conclusion that the antecedent also must be denied. Let's fill this form in with some content now:

If anyone is born of God, then he loves his brothers.	$B \supset L$
Adolph does not love his brothers.	$\sim L$
Therefore, Adolph is not born of God.	$\therefore \sim B$

Here the antecedent (or conditional) premise is stated first and the consequent is denied. In this case, although the antecedent is true, it is not true of Adolph. Our symbols convey this. B (= X is born of God) and L (= X loves his brothers), as such, are not denied, but showing L to be false in the case of Adolph leads to the conclusion that B is not true in his case either.

Another example of denying the consequent is seen in this difficult illustration. The trick here is that we need to deny a negative statement. Watch to see how this is done:

If logic does not apply to reality, then there cannot be any
    logical statements about reality.
There cannot be [no logical statements about reality].[1]
Therefore, logic does not [not apply to reality].

1. Even the statement "Logic does not apply to reality" is a logical statement about reality.

As you can see, the entire negative statement must be negated. Of course, no one really talks or writes like this. We just substitute an affirmative for a double negative, like, "Logic does apply to reality." Normally that is fine, but occasionally you can get into trouble doing that, so it is always best to spell out the double negative, at least in testing your argument. We used brackets here so that you could see the statement being denied. Symbols of this argument can show the original negative statements as positive characters or negative terms:

L ⊃ S	or	~L ⊃ ~S
~S		~[~S] = S
∴ ~L		∴ ~[~L] = L

Fallacies of Hypothetical Syllogisms

There are two ways to draw wrong conclusions from a hypothetical major premise. Both work against the causal relation implied in that premise. These are to deny the antecedent and to affirm the consequent. The problem in both fallacies is that the consequent might come about in some other way.

Denying the Antecedent. We usually only hear abbreviated versions of this fallacy that go something like, "Jesus is human, so he can't be God." This form is abbreviated because it states the denial of the consequent and the conclusion without stating the major premise. If we put it in hypothetical form, the argument would really be:

If Jesus is not human, then he is God.
Jesus is not [not human]. (i.e., he is human)
∴ Jesus is not God.

Now the fallacy becomes clear. The major premise says, "If not human, then God," not "If God, then not human." It tells us that if its antecedent is true its consequent also must be true; but it does not tell us that if its antecedent is false, its consequent also must be false. It leaves open the possibility that the consequent ("is God") might be true even while the antecedent ("is not human") is false. After all, Jesus might be (and in fact is) both God and man.

The point becomes more clear if we illustrate it with an argument not laden with such religious weight. Try this one on for size:

If Tom is not late for work, then he will attend the meeting.
Tom is not [not late for work]. (i.e., he is late for work)
Therefore Tom will not attend the meeting.

Why doesn't this argument hold water? Because there are other conditions under which Tom might still attend the meeting even if he is late for work. The other people in the meeting might agree to postpone it for him, for instance. Or Tom might be only a little bit late for work, but not late enough to miss the meeting. Whatever is the case, all that we're guaranteed by the first premise is that Tom will attend if he gets to work on time; we aren't guaranteed that he won't attend if he gets to work late. So the conclusion doesn't follow.

If you are going to deny something in a hypothetical syllogism, it had better be the consequent, not the antecedent. Just remember this simple rule: any hypothetical syllogism that depends on denying the antecedent is invalid, no matter how attractive it appears at first blush.

Affirming the Consequent. The second way to goof up a hypothetical syllogism is to affirm the consequent rather than the antecedent. When we affirm the antecedent, we guarantee the consequent. When we affirm the consequent, we guarantee nothing. Why? The same reason as before: the same consequent may have come about in some other way. Reincarnationists often make this error:

If reincarnation is true, then past-life regression therapy will work.
Past-life regression therapy works.
Therefore, reincarnation is true.

Past-life experiences brought out in such therapy may be pure imagination in some cases, self-induced guilt or role playing in others. The fact that the therapy works has nothing to do with the claims of reincarnation. People might just feel better if they can lay their feelings off on some imagined former self. The syllogism is not set up to handle the conclusion derived from it. To support the conclusion, the major premise would have to be reversed to "If past-life regression therapy works, then reincarnation is true." Then the form would be right, but you would have a problem proving that the major premise is true. You have to know that reincarnation is true before you can assert that it has any connection with past-life therapy.

The basic rule is this: *A valid hypothetical syllogism either denies the consequent (modus tollens) or affirms the antecedent (modus ponens) of the major premise; it doesn't deny the antecedent or affirm the consequent.*

Disjunctive Syllogisms

A strong disjunctive (or alternative) syllogism is one in which two alternatives (called alternants) are stated in the major premise, only one of which can be true.[2] In a strong disjunctive, it must be an "either/or" kind of sentence. The second premise must deny one of the alternants, and the conclusion must simply state the remaining term. These alternants might be single terms or entire propositions; it does not affect the form, which is the same for both:

Either P or Q	$P \vee Q$
Not Q	$\sim Q$
Therefore P	$\therefore P$

The symbol for *or* is a v-shaped wedge ($\vee$). This indicates the choice that must be made between the two alternants. It does not matter whether the first or second alternant is denied as long as one of them is. Why can't we *affirm* one alternant to eliminate the other? Simply because it is possible that both are true, even if they are true in different senses (as in weak disjunctives). You just can't be sure unless you already know that if one is true the other must be false. Even in cases where it is impossible for both terms of a disjunction to be true, affirming one alternant is really the same as denying the negative of the other.

Either God exists or God does not exist.
(Either God does not exist or God does not [not exist].)
God does not [not exist].
Therefore, God exists.

This trick can make the form valid, but it works only if it is really impossible for both alternants to be true. So even the

---

2. In a weak disjunction both may be true.

apparent exceptions follow the rules: you must deny one of the alternants in order for a disjunctive syllogism to be valid.

Moses gives an almost textbook example in Deuteronomy 30:15–19. He lays out the alternatives, negates one, and draws the conclusion:

> "See, I have set before you today life and prosperity, and death and adversity. . . ."
> "But if your heart turns away and you will not obey . . . I declare to you today that you will surely perish."
> "So choose life in order that you may live. . . ."

What could be more clear? You have a choice between life and death. You don't want to die. Therefore, choose life.

An argument that is disjunctive may give three alternatives. In this case, two must be denied to reach the conclusion.

> God is either uncaused, self-caused, or caused by another.
> It is impossible for a being to cause its own existence.
> God can't be caused by another, since he is the First Cause.
> Therefore, God is uncaused.

In short, if there are only three possible choices and two are false, then the third (and only remaining) choice must be true.

In his book, *Why I am not a Christian*, Bertrand Russell unwittingly provided a marvelous illustration of how *not* to use the disjunctive form. He affirmed one alternant rather than denying the other. He argued:

> Life was caused either by evolution or by design.
> Life was caused by evolution.
> Therefore, it was not caused by design (and so there is no reason to posit God).

This approach commits the formal fallacy of affirming one alternant. Even if the minor premise were true, the conclusion would not follow. For it is possible that both are true; that is, that evolution is designed.

Conjunctive Syllogisms

Disjunctive syllogisms are based on "either . . . or" sentences, but conjunctive syllogisms are used for "both . . . and" propositions. Conjunctive syllogisms are the only kind that yield two conclusions (or more) from only one premise! "How is such an incredible feat performed?" you ask. Much more easily than you might suppose, and it does not involve the use of mirrors. Watch closely.

Both P and Q are true.	P · Q
Therefore, P.	∴ P
Therefore, Q.	∴ Q

Presto! Aren't you amazed? By simply joining two terms in the premise, we can separate them and affirm each as a separate conclusion. (Notice our symbol for the conjunction *and* is a dot [·].) If both terms together are true, then each one separately is true also. This does not indicate any relation between the terms. They might have nothing at all to do with one another, but the fact that they are both true makes the syllogism valid.

So if we begin with "Christ is both fully God and fully man," then we can conclude that "Christ is fully God" and that "Christ is fully man." "Men are elected to salvation by God, and men have free will" also yields both of its components as conclusions. The same form may be followed for, "Roses are red, and violets are blue."

The interesting part of conjunctive syllogisms is what happens when we negate them. What does this mean: "Not [P and Q]"? Notice that the whole conjunct must be negated, since it is asserted as a whole. Does it mean that both P and Q are false, or only one of them? Of course, if both are false, the whole is false. But once we think about it, we see that if *either* term is false, then even if the other is true, the conjunct as a whole is false. If we say, "2 + 2 = 4 and 2 + 3 = 7," then the whole conjunct is false, because the conjunction rests on the truth of both its parts. So what conclusion can we reach from a negated conjunct? All we can say is that at least one of the premises is false, and maybe both are. In symbols, that comes out like this:

~(P · Q)
∴ ~P ∨ ~Q (and maybe ~P · ~Q)

Remember, conjuncts must be denied as a whole. If one part of the statement is false, then the conjunct is false *as a whole* (even if one part may happen to be true). So what would you expect the possible fallacy to be in this type of argument? That's right; the failure to negate one of the conjuncts. Both alternants must be true for the conjunct to be true as a whole. Thus, someone arguing against a conjunction need only show that at least one of the terms is false in order to show that the conjunct as a whole is not true.

For instance, the two crowning beliefs of the worldview of deism can be stated as the conjunct, "God exists and miracles are not possible." In order to show that this conjunct is false, at least one part of this conjunct must be negated. Theists would not wish to change the statement, "God exists," but they would rally arguments to show that the existence of a supernatural God who created the world automatically allows for the possibility of miracles. They would argue that if you agree that God created the world, you have already accepted the biggest miracle of all. Why not accept the lesser miracles also? Thus, they would negate the second half of the conjunct, "Miracles are not possible." The conclusion, then, is that the conjunct as a whole is false, and since the whole conjunct is necessary to describe deism, the worldview of deism is false. If it is not possible to negate one of the conjuncts, then there is no basis for denying the conjunct as a whole.

Dilemma Form of Syllogism

The dilemma form of argument is easily recognizable. Like a real-life dilemma, this type of reasoning attempts to force a person to affirm at least one of two positions, neither of which he wants to admit. A dilemma performs the much-needed and often exasperating job of making one think about the implications of what he believes. It does this by setting forth two hypothetical statements in its major premise, then stating as a disjunctive that one or the other of their antecedents is true. The conclusion then forces the person to choose between the consequents.

A Famous Dilemma

The famous French mathematician Blaise Pascal developed an argument that takes the form of a dilemma. Many have used it in evangelism without knowing its source, because it motivates people to make a decision. It can be stated like this:

If God exists, I have everything to gain by believing in him.
And if God does not exist, I have nothing to lose by believing in him.
Either God does exist or he does not exist.
Therefore, I have everything to gain or nothing to lose by believing in God.

The major premise simply spells out the implications that, if he exists, you had better be on his side, and if he doesn't, it doesn't matter—there is no judgment. The minor premise is key here because it narrows the field of possibilities to these two: either God exists or he doesn't. There are no third alternatives. That backs the person into a corner where he has to admit that belief in God is the reasonable and safest road to take, no matter what. Notice, though, that the conjunction in the conclusion has to be an *or*. To make that an *and* you would have to affirm that God both exists and does not exist at the same time. It might sound better, but it is logically impossible.

When we put the argument in symbolic form, we can see that it really handles two hypothetical syllogisms at once.

$$(P \supset Q) \cdot (R \supset S) \qquad\qquad (P \supset Q) \cdot (R \supset S)$$
$$P \vee R \qquad\qquad or \qquad\qquad \sim Q \vee \sim S$$
$$\therefore Q \vee S \qquad\qquad\qquad \therefore \sim P \vee \sim R$$

The fallacies possible in this form are the same as those of the hypothetical syllogisms, that is, denying the antecedent and affirming the consequent. Watch that minor premise! It might get sneaky and make one hypothetical valid and the other invalid (by affirming the antecedent of the first and the consequent of the second). In that case, the whole argument falls apart.

Jesus used a dilemma to silence his critics. In Mark 11:27–33, the story is told of how the religious leaders of Jerusalem questioned his authority. He answered their question with one of his own: "Was the baptism of John from heaven, or from men?" The scribes themselves spell out the dilemma:

"If we say 'From heaven,' He will say, 'Why did you not believe him?' But shall we say, 'From men'?"—they were afraid of the multitude, (for all considered John to have been a prophet indeed).

It was either from heaven or from men.
Therefore, either Jesus will condemn our unbelief or the multitude will attack us.

They simply chose to avoid the whole dilemma by saying, "We do not know." Rather than admit their unbelief, they chose to plead ignorance. This is not the best way to get out of a dilemma. It is much like Scarlet O'Hara's habit of avoiding tough choices by saying, "Oh fiddle-dee-dee, I'll think about that tomorrow." Neither approach makes any headway on the question, and problems don't go away that easily.

Avoiding Dilemmas
There are, however, three tactics that can be used to avoid a dilemma, even if it is formally valid. When you find your own views put on the horns of a dilemma, you can either "take the bull by the horns," (that is, dispute the implications of the major premise), "go between the horns" (show that there is a third alternative to the minor premise), or counter with another dilemma. So we can deny either the conjunction (the major premise) or the disjunction (the minor premise), respectively.

Going Between the Horns
Going between the horns is often the easiest way and is possible whenever the disjunction of the minor premise does not exhaust all logical possibilities. Now, our first example obviously covered all the logical possibilities: God either exists or does not, and there is no third alternative (pseudo-existence?). But in the second example, the scribes could have mentioned another possibility, that John's baptism came from hell. However, while logically possible, this only would have gotten them into more trouble with the people. Let's examine another argument:

If God willed the moral law arbitrarily, then he is not essentially good.
And if he willed it according to an ultimate standard beyond himself, then he is not God (because there is some ultimate beyond him).
But God willed the moral law either arbitrarily or according to an ultimate standard.
Therefore, either he is not good or he is not God.

The form of this argument is impeccable, but it is quite easy to go between its horns (i.e., to deny the minor premise) by asserting a third alternative. God could have willed moral law in accordance with his own goodness. He need not have resorted to anything beyond himself or to mere whim, but could have prescribed morality in accordance with the goodness of his own essence. The fact that theists believe God is essentially good is mentioned in the first premise, but somehow forgotten as an option in the second premise. If all logical possibilities are not accounted for, you can drive a truck between the horns of a dilemma.

Taking the Dilemma by the Horns

Another way of avoiding the conclusion drawn by a dilemma, when no third alternative is possible, is to take issue with the major premise itself. Are both of the "If . . . then," statements really true? Do their consequents really flow from their antecedents? Just raising doubt about one of them can invalidate the argument, because to deny a conjunction (which the first premise is), you only have to deny one of its members. Albert Camus describes a dilemma in his novel *The Plague*, in which a priest declares that the sickness is a judgment of God upon the people and chooses not to help the afflicted. The logic of the argument might be stated this way:

> If one helps the sick, then he is fighting against God, who sent the plague; and if one does not help the sick, then he is being cruel and inhumane.
> One must either help the sick or not help them.
> Therefore, one must either fight against God or be cruel and inhumane.

Here the minor premise wraps up all the logical possibilities; we can't go between these horns. Also, the latter half of the conjunction is hard to deny. It would indeed be cruel to refuse to help those in need (see 1 John 3:17). But it is possible to take this dilemma by the horns by denying the first half of the conjunction. The statement "God sent the plague" can be challenged on four counts. First, not all who suffer in natural disasters are being punished by God (Luke 13:3–4). Second, if the "plague" means the effects of sin on the whole fallen world, then God didn't send it. Man brought it on himself by his own free choice (Gen. 3:14; Rom. 5:12; 8:19–20). Third, it is never wrong to work against unjust suffering. If man brought evil into the world (through sin), then he can work to reverse the effects of evil (suffering) without worrying that he is fighting against God. Finally, the biblical theist is concerned not only with helping the victims of the plague, but also with treating it at the most effective level—its cause. He works to eliminate the *reason* for suffering, not just its *results*. The life-changing message of Christ's victory over sin and death is the most effective cure for evil known to man. It is better to eliminate the cause of the plague than simply to treat its symptoms. Thus, it is not true that fighting the plague means fighting against God. Having denied this part of the conjunction, the entire dilemma falls.

Countering the Dilemma

There is a third way to avoid a dilemma, a way that is intriguing and can enlighten others by offering a different perspective on problems: one can answer a dilemma with a counter-dilemma. When the conclusion of the first dilemma is unacceptable, a second dilemma sometimes can be offered that contradicts the conclusion of the first. This method will not prove or disprove anything for either side, because the two conclusions are not resolved and neither argument is shown to be invalid. It can, however, be effective when the original dilemma does not reveal the whole truth about a situation. Ideally, the counter-dilemma should consist of the same terms as the original, as is the case in the following:

> If I preach the gospel, I will displease some people, and if I do not preach the gospel, I will displease God.
> I either will or will not preach the gospel.
> Therefore, in either case, I will displease someone.

On the other hand,

> If I do not preach the gospel, some people will be pleased, and if I do preach the gospel, God will be pleased.
> I either will or will not preach the gospel.
> Therefore, in either case, I will please someone.

These two dilemmas offset each other. To reach a conclusion in this discussion it must be shown that it is better to be loved by God than by men, which is a very different argument. The point here is that a counterdilemma can show that more than one conclusion can follow from the same terms in some cases. However, either of the first two methods for avoiding dilemmas is preferable.

Sorites

The last type of syllogism we need to look at is called a *sorites*. The word comes from a Greek word *(soros)* meaning "a heap." This is a pretty accurate description of the argument, which heaps up premises that all link together. It is a series of syllogisms telescoped into an argument. An example is worth a thousand words here (Rom. 5:3–5):

All who suffer persevere.
All who persevere develop character.
All who develop character have hope.
All who have hope will not be disappointed.
All who are not disappointed can rejoice.
Therefore, all who suffer can rejoice.

If you take any two consecutive premises from this argument, they form a perfect syllogism that follows all the rules we stated in the last chapter. The trick is to link them all together so that *the predicate of the preceding premise is always the subject of the following one.* With this seamless web, the subject of the very first premise (All who suffer) leads to the predicate of the very last (rejoice) and these become the conclusion.

Paul must have liked sorites, because he put another one in chapter eight of Romans, where he wrote, "For whom He foreknew, He also predestined [to become] conformed to the image of His Son, that He might be the first-born among many brethren; and whom He predestined, these He also called; and whom He called, these He also justified; and whom He justified, these He also glorified" (vv. 29–30). Though he does not state his conclusion formally, it is clear that all whom God foreknew will be glorified (see v. 28).

There are three criteria that must be met for a sorites to be valid: 1. The subject of each premise must be the same as the predicate of the one before it. Otherwise there is no middle term that carries the logic through. 2.The conclusion must be constructed of the subject of the first premise and the predicate of the last. If either of these rules is broken, the argument can be dismissed as formally invalid. 3.In addition to these, this argument must meet the expectations of all seven rules of the syllogism when each pair of premises in the series is broken down.

Symbolically, a sorites will look like this:

$A < B$		$A \supset B$
$B < C$	*or*	$B \supset C$
$C < D$ (etc.)		$C \supset D$
$\therefore\ A < D$		$\therefore\ A \supset D$

Enthymeme

Here is a word you may never have heard, but you see enthymemes all the time. They are not compound syllogisms, but we didn't have any place else to discuss them. Actually, an enthymeme is almost the opposite of a compound syllogism. Rather than adding premises, it takes them away. It is used in most of the logical arguments you read every day in newspapers, magazines, advertisements, and textbooks.

An enthymeme is simply a sawed-off syllogism. It is a standard syllogism stated with one part missing (usually one of the premises). Most of the time, a writer wants you to know his conclusion and gives some reason to support it, but he assumes that you already know the other premise. In fact, the name comes from a Greek phrase meaning "in the mind." When an ad man writes, "You should buy our cereal because we have 20 percent more oat bran," he expects you to know that oat bran can reduce serum cholesterol, that this will reduce your risk of heart attack, that not having a heart attack is good for health, that health is good for man, and that man is a good thing in itself. He only stated his conclusion and one premise and expected you to fill in the other three premises on your own. But it worked, didn't it?

The enthymeme relies on the logical nature of the human mind to do its job and fill in the missing information. Formally, this can take any valid form of syllogism, so we can't prescribe any symbolic language to it, except that something is missing from the form. For example, Paul wrote, "Death came to all men, because all sinned (Rom. 5:12)." In syllogistic form, this turns out to be a categorical syllogism with the major premise missing:

[All men who sin die.] (implied premise)
All men sinned.
Therefore, all men died.

This type of argument need not have a logical fallacy, but enthymemes can hide fallacies in their unstated premises. Also, if you are going to use an enthymeme, make sure that the missing premise really is understood by your audience. If not, you'll be like the comic who tried to salvage a joke by going back to explain, "Did I mention that the duck was wearing pants?"

That's it. These are the forms of argument that are used in deductive logic. When you break it down, it gets pretty easy to remember. There are two types of hypothetical syllogisms (modus ponens and modus tollens), disjunctive and conjunctive syllogisms, dilemmas, enthymemes (abbreviations), and sorites (heaps). The symbols aren't so hard to remember either.

⊃ (horseshoe)	if . . . then
∨ (wedge)	either . . . or
· (raised dot)	and
~ (negation)	not
∴ (conclusion)	therefore
<	is (are)
≮	is (are) not

Piece of cake, right? The real question is, would you know one if it bit you? You can find these forms of arguments in the books you read, in conversation with friends, or in the news stories and advertisements that are trying to influence the decisions you make every day. Chapter seven will help you learn to do that. But first, now that you know what makes an argument good, it is time to find out what can make it bad. That is the subject of the next two chapters.

Exercises for Chapter 4

4.1 Put the following hypothetical arguments into symbolic logic. Determine if they are using *modus ponens* or *modus tollens* and if they are either valid or invalid. If any are invalid, explain which fallacy they are committing.

1. If God exists, then man has meaning in life.
   Man has meaning in life.
   God must exist.

2. If Christ did not rise from the dead, then we are lost in our sins. (1 Cor. 15:17)
   It is not the case that Christ did not rise from the dead.
   We are not lost in our sins.

3. If the Bible is the word of God, then it is inerrant.
   The Bible is the word of God.
   It is inerrant.

4. Sally will go to church, if she becomes a Christian.
   Sally went to church.
   She became a Christian.

5. If evolution is true, then the second law of thermodynamics is wrong.
   But the second law of thermodynamics is not wrong.
   Evolution is not true.

6. Christ deceived the apostles concerning his resurrection, if he did not rise in the same physical body he died in.
   Christ cannot deceive the apostles concerning his resurrection.
   Christ rose in the same body he died in.

7. If two propositions contradict, then they both can't be true.
   These two propositions don't contradict.
   They both must be true.

8. If the antecedent is affirmed in a hypothetical syllogism, then it is valid.
   The antecedent is affirmed in this hypothetical syllogism.
   It is valid.

9. There must be a necessary being, if the universe has a cause.
   The universe has a cause.
   There must be a necessary being.

10. If God exists, then miracles are possible.
    Miracles are possible.
    God must exist.

4.2 Put the following disjunctive syllogisms into symbolic logic. Determine if they are either valid or invalid. If any are invalid, explain the fallacy being committed.

1. Either God exists or he doesn't exist.
   It is not the case that God doesn't exist.
   God exists.
2. Either Jesus rose from the dead or he is not God.
   Jesus rose from the dead.
   He is God.
3. Either God exists or evil exists.
   Evil exists.
   God doesn't exist.
4. Either the law of entropy is not true or the universe had a beginning.
   The law of entropy is not `not true.'
   The universe had a beginning.
5. Either Christ fulfilled the prophecies concerning the Messiah or the Bible is untrustworthy.
   Christ fulfilled prophecies concerning the Messiah.
   The Bible is trustworthy.

4.3 Put the following dilemmas into symbolic logic. Determine if they are constructive or destructive. Then determine if they are valid or invalid. If any are invalid, explain the fallacy being committed.

1. If you trust Christ, then you will go to heaven, and if you don't trust Christ, then you will go to hell.
   But, either you trust Christ or you don't.
   So either you go to heaven or you go to hell.
2. If atheism is true, then there is no possibility for meaning in life, and if theism is true, then there is the potential for a meaningful life.
   There is either no meaning in life or there does exist the potential for a meaningful life.
   So either atheism is true or theism is true.
3. If the conclusion of a syllogism just states something already given in the premises, then it adds nothing to our knowledge and is useless, and if the conclusion states something not contained in the premises, then it is invalid.

So, either the conclusion just states something already given in the premises, or it states something not contained in the premises.

Therefore all syllogisms are either useless or invalid.

4. If the Bible can be trusted, then Jesus rose from the dead, and if Jesus did not rise from the dead, then we have no hope for salvation.

   This means that either the Bible can be trusted or there is no hope for salvation.

   So either Christ rose from the dead or he didn't.

5. If evil exists, then God cannot be omnipotent, and if evil exists, then he cannot be omnibenevolent.

   However, it is not true either that God is not omnipotent or that he is not omnibenevolent.

   So evil doesn't exist.

6. If there is morality, then there must be a moral law maker, and if there is a moral law maker, then there is a God.

   Either there is a moral law maker or there isn't one.

   Hence either there is morality or there is no God.

7. If God exists, then his existence is necessary, and if he doesn't exist, then his existence is impossible.

   Either God exists or he doesn't exist.

   Therefore his existence is either necessary or impossible.

8. If Jesus is God, then he fulfilled prophecy, and if Jesus is God, then he performed miracles.

   It is not the case that Jesus either fulfilled prophecy or performed miracles.

   So, Jesus is not God.

9. If atheists are not wise, then Christians are, and if the Bible is the source of wisdom, then those who do not read it will not be wise.

   Either Christians are wise or those who don't read the Bible won't be wise.

   Hence, either atheists are wise or the Bible is the source of wisdom.

10. If those who attend church regularly grow spiritually, then it vindicates church attendance, and if those who read their Bible regularly grow spiritually, then it vindicates Bible reading.

    However, neither church attendance nor Bible reading has been vindicated.

So, neither attending church nor reading the Bible helps spiritual growth.

4.4 Return to the above dilemmas. For those that are valid, suggest a refutation for them by either going between the horns, taking the dilemma by the horns, or countering the dilemma.

4.5 In the following enthymemes, determine whether the missing statement is a premise or conclusion. Then supply the missing proposition, attempting to create a valid syllogism, if possible. If it is not possible, explain why the syllogism is invalid.

1. Pro-lifers should break the law and block the doors of abortion clinics, because they are saving lives.
2. Jesus Christ did miracles and only someone sent by God can do miracles.
3. If Christianity is not of God, it will die out.
   Christianity has not died out.
4. Some believers will suffer loss at the judgment seat of Christ, however all believers will be saved.
5. I know that God exists because something must have started all of this.
6. To be a Christian you must believe in the bodily resurrection.
   Bultmann does not believe in the bodily resurrection.
7. God loves all men and desires that every man be saved.
8. Deism teaches that God does not intervene in the world.
   But, it is true that Jesus Christ is God.
9. Some believers grow spiritually because of their church attendance, and all Christians go to church.
10. I believe nature was created by intelligence, because nature is complexly designed.

4.6. Determine if the following sorites are valid or invalid, and if invalid explain the fallacy being committed.

1. No P < Q
   Q < S
   S < T
   No P < T
2. All Christians are Bible believers.
   Some Bible believers are church attenders.

No church attenders are immoral.
No Christians are immoral.

3. Some people do not believe in God.
   All who do not believe in God sleep in on Sunday morning.
   All who sleep in on Sunday morning miss church.
   Some people miss church.

4. Some K < L
   No L < non-M
   Some non-M ⊀ non-N
   Non-N < O
   Some K < O

5. Miracles are possible.
   Natural events are not miracles.
   The birth of babies is a natural event.
   The birth of a baby is not a miracle.

6. Some philosophers are Christians.
   All Christians are going to heaven.
   All who are going to heaven are happy.
   Some philosophers are happy.

7. Wayne needs proof of God's existence.
   Proof of God's existence can be reasoned through natural arguments.
   Reasons given through natural argument are not guarantees that someone will believe.
   Wayne is not a person who is guaranteed to believe.

8. A < B
   B < C
   C < D
   No D < E
   No B < E

9. Some Christians reject theistic proofs.
   Those who reject theistic proofs are sometimes called fideists.
   Not all those who are called fideists are really fideists.
   Some Christians are not really fideists.

10. Some X < Y
    Y < Z
    Every Z needs L.
    All who need L are P.
    However, No P < M
    Some X is not M.

5

Formal Fallacies

Since you now know what you need to know about how to do logic right, it is time you learned how to recognize bad logic. *Fallacy* is a general term referring to anything that can possibly go wrong in a logical argument. It is important to know fallacies because even though they might be psychologically persuasive, they are not logically correct. They cause people to accept conclusions for inadequate reasons. By knowing fallacies, we can specify why an argument is faulty. But knowing fallacies is not only a help in refuting error; it also protects us from criticism and gives us the ability to develop clearer expression of our thoughts.

Many of the examples used in this chapter may be familiar to you. Some come from the Bible. Some come from the secular philosophers whose arguments are widely used on college campuses today. Others come from theologians, and still others from *Reader's Digest*. You probably won't remember the names of all these fallacies, but you should be able to recognize a problem next time you encounter a faulty argument.

There are two kinds of fallacies: formal and informal. No, you don't have to be wearing jeans to a prom to commit a formal fallacy. *Formal fallacies* are *errors in the way an argument is put together.* They have to do with the relationships between propositions and the construction of the argument. We met each of these when we discussed syllogisms, but will list them here for handy reference. *Informal fallacies* are *errors in clarity or soundness of the reasoning process.* We will study them in Chapter 6.

Fallacies of the Categorical Syllogism

Categorical syllogisms are the backbone of logical structures. We looked at them in chapter 2. It might be a good idea to look back at them again, since it is hard to know what is the wrong way to do something unless we understand the right way. Fallacies are like counterfeits: you can't recognize a counterfeit unless you know the genuine.

Illicit Major. The major term is distributed in the conclusion but not in the premise.

All who are trusting in Jesus are saved.
Harry is not trusting in Jesus.
Harry is not saved.

This syllogism looks right, but in fact it is invalid. This is because our major term, *saved*, is undistributed in the premise but distributed in the conclusion. In the first premise, *saved* refers only to *some* members of the group of saved persons (the ones who are trusting in Jesus). But when we arrive at the conclusion, *saved* refers to the entire group of saved persons. You cannot logically conclude anything about a whole group from something you only know about part of it, even if it looks right. Remember, we are interested in the structure or form of a syllogism at this point, not in its truthfulness.

Another way to see this fallacy is through the moods and figures we learned in Chapter 3. This syllogism is an AEE mood in the first figure. What does the chart (Figure 3.1) say about its validity? Just remember: you can never have a type A proposition for a major premise and a type E for the conclusion or else you will commit the fallacy of illicit major.

Illicit Minor. The minor term is distributed in the conclusion but not in the premises.

All murder is sin.
All sin is willful disobedience.
Therefore, all willful disobedience is murder.

In this case, the minor premise talks about all sin, but not about all willful disobedience. But the conclusion speaks of all willful disobedience. Again, this mood (AAA) is not valid in the fourth figure.

Illicit Middle. The middle term is not distributed at least once. (This fallacy is also called Undistributed Middle.)

All angels are immortal.
All saints are immortal.
Therefore, all saints are angels.

This is the kind of reasoning Hollywood has used to make all those movies about people who become angels. But the extent of the term *immortal* is never wrapped up in the premises. God is immortal too, but we wouldn't try to say that all men are God. By the way, want to guess what the figure and mood chart says about this one?

Four-Term Fallacy. There are more than three terms in an argument.

Orthodox Christianity teaches that evil does not exist in itself.
Christian Science teaches that evil does not exist.
Therefore, Christian Science is orthodox Christianity.

At least one defender of Mary Baker Eddy, founder of Christian Science, has used this kind of argument, and others use it to defend New Age beliefs. The problem is that there is a grand equivocation in the middle term. That is to say, it is being used in two different ways. It is one thing to say that evil really does not exist *in itself*, but quite another to say that it does not exist *at all*. Orthodox Christians teach that evil exists as a corruption or privation in something else. It is a lack of some good thing that ought to be there. (For instance, blindness is a lack of sight, and rape a lack of love.) So the word *evil* in the phrases "evil does not exist in itself" and "evil does not exist" constitutes two terms, not one. The middle term is not a point of agreement at all, but the very matter that separates the two views.

Fallacies of the Hypothetical Syllogism

Denying the Antecedent. The error here is in overly emphasizing the causal connection implied in the first premise. Just because A implies B does not mean that B cannot be without A. Something else might also cause B.

If miracles are possible, then God exists.
Miracles are not possible.
Therefore, God does not exist.

Though some atheists have used a similar argument, it is possible that some other good reason to believe in God might be found (such as the need for an uncaused cause of a caused universe).

Affirming the Consequent. This method also confuses the causal connection in the first premise by telling us that the consequent is true without confirming that the antecedent caused it. There might be some other cause. "If and only if" language can avoid this fallacy. An overzealous churchman might argue:

If God exists, then miracles are possible.
Miracles are happening (at so-and-so's church, on television, etc.).
Therefore, God exists.

The argument looks attractive, but it is fallacious. It affirms the consequent, not the antecedent. The only way to make this valid is to show that only God can perform miracles (a tough job when demonic miracles are cited in the New Testament). It's better to abandon this argument entirely and prove that God exists on other grounds.

The Fallacy of the Disjunctive Syllogism

Affirming One Alternant. By affirming only one alternant of a weak disjunction, we really don't know anything about the other alternant. We can't deny what we know nothing about. To deny an alternant, we have to deny it, not just affirm the other one.

Either the universe was created by God or it evolved.
Evolution is true.
Therefore, the universe was not created by God.

Even if evolution were true, it would not eliminate the possibility of creation. It is always possible that God could have used evolution as a means of creating. The falsity of one statement cannot be proven by the truth of another unless they actually contradict or are contraries (see the Square of Opposition in Chapter 3). Where the disjunctive syllogism does contain a disjunct with mutually exclusive alternants (i.e., "either dead or alive"), it should be treated as an enthymeme. In other words, ignore the disjunct. For example:

Christ is either dead or alive.
Christ is alive.
Therefore, Christ is not dead.

Here the disjunct is superfluous because if Christ is alive, he can't be dead. Therefore, you can simply ignore the disjunct and treat this as an enthymeme.

The Fallacy of Conjunctive Syllogisms

Conjunctive syllogisms suffer from the same fallacies as weak disjunctive syllogisms: affirming one alternant. The following is a conjunctive fallacy of affirming one alternant:

Methodists both sprinkle babies and worship on Sundays.
Methodists sprinkle babies.
Therefore, Methodists do not both sprinkle babies and worship on Sundays.

This conclusion obviously does not follow from the premises, since it has not negated part of the conjunct in order to make the conjunct as a whole false.

Fallacies of Other Types of Syllogisms

All of the fallacies of other forms of the syllogism have been covered by what we have already done. For example, a dilemma is really a hypothetical syllogism with a twist, so its fallacies are the same: denying the antecedent and affirming the consequent. We are left with sorites.

All who are saved go to heaven.
All who go to heaven see God.
All who see God will be eternally happy. Therefore, all who are saved will be eternally happy.

Sorites can be tricky, since they can have so many premises. There are several problems that might arise. First, the subject of each premise must be the same as the predicate of the one before it. Without that, there is no middle term that carries the logic through.

Second, the conclusion must be constructed of the subject of the first premise and the conclusion of the last premise. If either of these rules is broken, the argument can be dismissed as formally invalid.

Third, in addition to these, this argument is expected to meet the expectations of all seven rules of the syllogism when each pair of premises in the series is broken down.

See if you can find all three types of problems in this sorites before you look at the footnote.[1]

1. Abortion is legal.
2. What is legal is good.
3. What is good is good for persons.
4. Women are persons.
5. Persons have rights.
6. Therefore, women have a right to abortion.

Practice Makes Perfect

Logic is like music—practice makes perfect. The only way you can be sure you really understand these fallacies is to see if you can spot them in action. Look at the following exercises and determine what, if anything, is wrong. It's actually fun to find the fallacy!

Exercises for Chapter 5

5.1 Below are several examples of all the different kinds of syllogisms we have examined thus far. First identify the type of syllogism. Then determine if any of the fallacies mentioned in this chapter are being committed and, if so, which ones.

1. Either we should believe in God or we should become nihilists.
   We shouldn't become nihilists.
   We should believe in God.
2. No child abusers are just.
   Some atheists are just.
   No atheists are child abusers.

1. First, the subject of the conclusion (women) is not the subject of the first premise (rather, abortion is). Second the predicate of premise 3 (persons) is not the subject of premise 4 (rather, women is). Third, it violates one of the rules of a syllogism; this is the fallacy of an undistributed middle term (persons).

3. $(B \supset A) \cdot (C \supset D)$
   $\sim(A \lor D)$
   $\sim(B \lor C)$
4. $S < P$
   $Q < P$
   $\therefore S < Q$
5. If the resurrection is not true, then we are lost in our sins.
   It is not the case that the resurrection is not true.
   We are not lost in our sins.
6. No $A < B$.
   $B < C$
   $C < D$
   Some $D < E$
   $\therefore$ No $A < E$.
7. If the cosmological argument is true, then a personal God exists, and if the universe is eternal, then the universe is God.
   Either the cosmological argument is true or the universe is eternal.
   Therefore, either a personal God exists or the universe is God.
8. God loves all men.
   All men are sinners.
   Therefore, God loves sinners.
9. $J \supset Q$
   Q
   $\therefore J$
10. It is true that Jesus both deliberately tried to fulfill prophecy and is just a man.
    Jesus is not just a man.
    So, it is not true that Jesus both deliberately tried to fulfill prophecy and is just a man.
11. Man is completely free.
    God is not a man.
    Hence, God is not completely free.
12. $(N \supset L) \cdot (\sim N \supset S)$
    $L \lor S$
    $\therefore N \lor \sim N$
13. No contingent being is necessary.
    God is necessary.
    So, God is not a contingent being.

14. Archaeology supports the Bible.
    That which supports the Bible is a good apologetic tool.
    All good apologetic tools should be vigorously studied.
    Anything that should be vigorously studied will be hard work.
    Hard work is no fun.
    Hence, archaeology is no fun.
15. Either every effect has a cause or some effects are uncaused.
    Every effect has a cause.
    So, it is not the case that some effects are uncaused.
16. S < M
    Some M < P
    ∴ Some S < P
17. If Jesus were God, then he would appear whenever I asked.
    However, Jesus doesn't appear whenever I ask.
    Hence, Jesus is not God.
18. George believes that Paul is truthful.
    Paul believes in Jesus Christ.
    Therefore George believes in Jesus Christ.
19. If deism is true, then the Bible cannot be true.
    Deism is false.
    So, the Bible can be true.
20. Z < G
    Some L < Z
    ∴ L < G.
21. B ∨ O
    ~O
    ∴ B
22. If intelligence only comes from intelligence, then evolution can't be true.
    Evolution can't be true.
    Hence, intelligence only comes from intelligence.
23. (J ⊃ K) · (F ⊃ R)
    J ∨ F
    ∴ K ∨ R
24. All humanists are interested in human rights.
    No Christian is a humanist.
    Therefore, no Christian is interested in human rights.

25. If you are a student of logic, then you can determine if syllogisms are valid or invalid, and if you are a student of the Bible, then you can explain a passage of Scripture to someone.

    Either you can determine if syllogisms are valid or invalid, or you can explain a passage of Scripture to someone.

    So, either you are a student of logic or a student of the Bible.

26. No B < T
    Some T < V
    ∴ Some V ⊀ B

27. $(U \lor I) \cdot (E \lor O)$
    $(E \lor O)$
    ∴ $(U \lor O) \cdot (E \lor O)$

28. In your faith you should supply moral excellence, and in your moral excellence, knowledge; and in your knowledge, self-control; and in your self-control, perseverance; and in your perseverance, godliness; and in your godliness, brotherly kindness; and in your brotherly kindness, Christian love. (2 Pet. 1:5–7)

    So, your faith should supply Christian love.

29. $(C \lor D) \supset H$
    $\sim(C \lor D)$
    $\sim H$

30. Either these exercises are over or you have to do some more.

    These exercises are over.

    Therefore, you do not have to do any more.

6

Informal Fallacies

At first blush you might think that an informal fallacy is the failure to wear a tux to your best friend's wedding. But it isn't. It is an error in clarity or soundness of thought. Informal fallacies are any errors in reasoning not related to the *form* of the syllogism. They relate to whether the propositions have any bearing on the case at hand. The formal validity of the argument is not in question here; truth is. Do the statements supply evidence for the claim being made?

Different authors have given different answers to the question of how many fallacies there are. Aristotle listed only thirteen, but one modern author lists 112! It's really impossible to say how many ways people can find to make mistakes.

Under the heading of informal fallacies, there are two basic types of errors: *fallacies of ambiguity* (where the meaning of the statements is not clear) and *fallacies of relevance* (where the meaning is clear, but it does not address the right issues of the argument).

Fallacies of relevance can be divided again into causal and

Figure 6.1

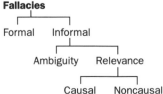

noncausal types. The first kind is found only in inductive arguments, where causal connections are being established, so we will discuss them in chapter 10, after the section on induction. Here we will only concern ourselves with the noncausal type. The chart in Figure 6.1 may help you understand this organization of the different kinds of fallacies.

Fallacies of Ambiguity

There are many ways to be ambiguous and they are all dangerous to clear communication. In fact, ambiguity is one of the seven deadly sins of correct thinking. Ambiguity is divided into four basic categories: simple ambiguity, amphibole, ambiguity of accent, and ambiguity of circumstance.

Simple Ambiguity (or equivocation). Simple ambiguity occurs when a word or phrase is used with two or more meanings. In other words, it is an equivocation on the meaning of a term or phrase. Consider these examples:

"If all men are created equal, then why are pro basketball players so tall?"
"Your argument is sound; nothing but sound."

It is clear that the phrase *created equal* has more than one meaning in the first example. In one instance it means the same height; in the other it refers to moral and political rights. Likewise, in the second example, the word *sound* means a good argument in one case and a pointless or empty one in the other.

Amphibole (or relationship). The ambiguity of amphibole is one where the words are clear but the grammatical construction is not. You can't tell for sure how to relate the parts of the sentences:

"Save soap and waste paper."
or,
"I live by the river; drop in some time."
or,
"The airplane took off slowly with Mary on it, her nose hugging the ground."

In each case, the words used can be seen in two different relationships (just as an amphibian can live in two different contexts, land and water). Is "waste" an adjective or a verb? Drop in to see him at his home or drop into the river? Was it the airplane's nose or Mary's that was hugging the ground? (In English grammar this is a dangling participle as well as a dangling nose.) Confusion like this in serious communication can lead to havoc in the logic of the argument.

Accent (or emphasis). Ambiguity of accent occurs when the accent, emphasis, or tone of voice changes the meaning.

> "You have heard that it was said, `You shall love your *neighbor*, and hate your enemy'" [Matt. 5:43].

This is a classic example of Pharisaic reasoning on the law. They figured that if the Law only said you had to love your neighbor, then it was okay to hate other people. Jesus corrected this in Matthew 5:44 with, "But I say to you, love your enemies and pray for those who persecute you."

Even the simple words "I love you" can have the reverse meaning when said with a different emphasis:

> "I love *you*?"
> "*I* love you?"
> "I love you."
> "I *love* you?"

You have to be careful, not only in what you say, but how you say it. And if you are going to say these three magic words, then you have to be careful to whom you say them!

Significance (or circumstance). The ambiguity of significance is committed when conditions or circumstances change the meaning of the words. It is one thing for a child to look into the bowl of his grandfather's pipe and say, "Fire in the hole." It is quite another for a man at an excavation site to yell, "Fire in the hole!" to warn everyone that explosives are about to be detonated. Likewise, a student may ask his philosophy professor, "What is truth?" and the meaning is certainly different from the same words uttered by Pontius Pilate.

In dealing with non-Christians, it is easy to see that the context of world views can also change the meanings of words. The term *Son of God* means very different things to a Christian (God incarnate), a Jehovah's Witness (the highest created being), and a New Ager (God in all men). The term *creation* also evokes various interpretations, from a poetic image of evolution, to emanations of God, to making something from nothing. The belief systems behind the words a person uses can change the words' meaning radically.

Fallacies of Relevance: Errors that Don't Address the Issues

There are many ways to bring irrelevant matters into a discussion, and this list is not intended to be complete. These fallacies show that people will go to any length to win an argument, even if they can't prove their point. When backed into a corner, debaters can be more dangerous than a wild animal. We will look at how they might respond in several categories. They might attack not your argument, but *you!* They might try any ploy to appeal to some inappropriate authority, like emotions, ignorance, or even how old your argument is. Or they might stack the deck. It is easier to refute a view when you arrange to have all the answers come out your way. Others prefer just to change the subject. Finally, they might teach you to ignore all differences. After all, where there are no differences, there is agreement and the argument is over. Don't fall for it! These are all just games to avoid the real issues. They are irrelevant, and that's why they are wrong.

Attack!

Argument ad Baculum (appeal to force). This type of argument does not even attempt to be relevant. It simply says, "Accept this argument, or I'll beat you up!" It seeks to persuade by force. It is a threat, reasoning through blackmail, argument by intimidation. It assumes that might makes right. What does that have to do with logic?

> ". . . they had nothing to say in reply. . . . And when they had threatened them further, they let them go (finding no basis on which they might punish them). . . . and after calling the apostles in, they flogged them and ordered them to speak no more in the name of Jesus. . . ." [Acts 4:14, 21; 5:40]

Argumentum ad Hominem (abusive). This is argument by character assassination. "Reject whatever he says because he is a bad person." Literally, the fallacy's name means "argument against the man." It is not an attack on the *proposition,* but against the *person.* It is like a lawyer standing up and saying, "We have no case, your honor; but certainly you're not going to believe the alcoholic, El Sleazo, ambulance chaser that the plaintiff hired."

> "Behold, a gluttonous man and a drunkard, a friend of tax-gatherers and sinners!" [Matt. 11:19]
> "Kubler-Ross's views on the stages of grief should be rejected because she has contact with departed spirits."

It should be noted here that whether the accusations are true or not makes no difference, since the argument is irrelevant. Even if Kubler-Ross has had contact with "departed spirits," her work on the grief process (which has been verified by others) is still helpful. Jesus' claim to be God was in no way diminished by the fact that he associated with sinners. These attacks are simply ways to dodge the issues.

Argumentum ad Hominem (circumstantial). Sound familiar? Same song; second verse. This time, the argument is not an assault on the man's character, but on some special circumstances surrounding him. This form of the fallacy occurs in the following:

> Why should we believe Solomon when he tells us to be satisfied with "the wife of your youth" (Prov. 5:18)? He wasn't.

Here it is seen as *inconsistent* for Solomon to be giving advice on marriage when he had seven hundred wives and three hundred concubines. Isn't it nice to know that God uses imperfect people? Who would know the problems of marital infidelity better than Solomon? Besides, if all the writers of Scripture had to be perfect, we would have no Bible! Paul and Moses were murderers, Matthew was a tax-gatherer, and Peter had denied the Lord, but God used them all. The circumstances may seem inconsistent, but that does not change the truth of the propositions they uttered. The objection is irrelevant.

> "Why should we believe this expert witness's testimony about creation science, since he believes that some UFO experiences are a Satanic manifestation?

This time the attack is against *other beliefs* that the man holds. Even though UFOs have nothing to do with his testimony, these special circumstances are used to discredit him. This does not change the validity of his testimony in the least. In fact, it does not even address his testimony. It is not relevant to the argument at all. The same error is made by those who argue against the pro-life movement, home schooling, and other positions by saying, "Their supporters are religious people." The fact that they have other beliefs does not alter the truth of what they say about these issues.

Special case: The weight of the testimony of a witness in a court might be diminished if it is shown that the man is a chronic liar, but it does not mean that his testimony is *false*, only that it is not *credible*. There may be other witnesses who testify to the same thing and are reliable. Many logicians have made a big to-do about Paul's statement in Titus 1:12 that a Cretan said, "All Cretans are liars." It can't be true, they say, because if a Cretan said it, he was lying; but if he was telling the truth, then the statement is false. But Paul assures us that the statement is true. After all, the poet didn't say that Cretans *always* lie, just that Cretans *all* lie sometimes.

Inappropriate Authorities

Some fallacies lead us to think that we should believe something other than the reasoning that is presented in the argument. They ask us to look at our emotions, evaluate our own ignorance before passing judgment, believe a famous name, or reverence new ideas. These use our sense of being subject to authority to derail our thinking. Usually, such appeals have nothing to do with the argument at hand.

Argumentum ad Ignorantiam (argument from ignorance). This type of thinking assumes that something should be believed until it is shown to be false. One who uses this fallacy says, "Accept this because you can't prove it isn't true." In other words, if you don't know something is wrong, you should embrace it. But what would happen if someone approached a snake with the attitude of, "Well, I can't prove that it is poisonous, so I guess it's safe to pick it up"?

There is a place for closed-mindedness. Propositions, unlike defendants in a court of law, are not presumed true (innocent) until proven false (guilty). Ignorance proves nothing, and all that can be concluded from nothing is nothing.

Atheist: "There can't be a God, because I have never seen any evidence for him."

Christian: "There must be a God, because no one can prove that he doesn't exist."

Only God knows how many arguments have ended in this stalemate. The problem is that both parties are wrong. Neither view should be accepted on the basis of ignorance. That is no way to find truth! Let positive evidence be presented and evaluated for both sides, and the truth can be known. As Aquinas said, "the contrary of a truth can never be demonstrated." If a conclusion is false, it is only a matter of finding the fallacy or the untrue premises (or both). Don't stop looking for the light while you are still in the dark.

N.B. An argument from silence is not always an argument from ignorance, especially when the context demands a specific conclusion. For example, in Acts 1:6–7, the disciples ask Christ if the time had come to restore the Kingdom to Israel. His answer was, "It is not for you to know times or epochs." Some have concluded that this means that Christ did not believe the kingdom would come. However, an argument from silence would respond, "Then why didn't he say, `I don't believe there will be an earthly kingdom,' instead?" This argument rests on a rather loud silence that demands only one answer: He did believe in an earthly kingdom, but told the disciples that they did not need to know when it was coming.

Argumentum ad Misericordiam (appeal to pity). Here is a classic emotional appeal: "If this man is given the death sentence, who will take care of his wife and children?" "I don't want to go to heaven knowing that I have loved ones suffering in hell." This kind of argument says, "Accept this because you should feel pity (or sympathy) for the one involved." This is often the appeal for people who object to eternal damnation saying, "What about the deaf, blind, mentally retarded, aborigine infant in Africa who has not heard the gospel?"

This was also the appeal of the man who responded to Jesus' call by saying, "Permit me first to go and bury my father" (Luke. 9:59). He thought Jesus would surely honor such a request. But Jesus cut right through the irrelevance of it and emphasized the importance of preaching the gospel (the relevant matter).

There is an exception to this rule: when the conclusion reached is not a factual matter, but only a matter of sentiment. In such cases, a sentimental appeal is quite appropriate.

Argumentum ad Populum. This is the fallacy of deciding truth by opinion polls. It says, "Accept this because it has popular appeal." It is the kind of argument that plays to the galleries, not to the facts. It is an attempt to win by fashionable ideas, not by good arguments. These arguments have "snob appeal" because they agree with an elite or select group and demand that everybody jump on the bandwagon. Hey, it worked for Hitler!

"Only an IGNORAMUS would reject this."
"God is love; so just love everybody and don't worry about judgment."
"Since the inerrancy of Scripture is a divisive doctrine, we should reject it."
"A woman has a right to control her own body; so she has the right to abort the baby in her body."

In each case above, a popular concept has been used to make people accept an idea that they may not be sure about. The truth of the propositions is not addressed at all. Why can't a loving God lovingly allow people to choose their own destiny? Why can't the church be unified by believing in inerrancy? Why can't a woman control her body by not getting pregnant? The arguments sidestep the issue by wielding the authority of public opinion. The next fallacy is similar.

Consensus Gentium. "Accept this because most people believe it is true." While the argument *ad populum* may have only appealed to a minority trend, the *consensus gentium* requires a majority opinion. So this is deciding truth by majority vote. Often this sounds good because we agree with the majority, but we just might all be wrong. Most of us have enough people-pleaser in us to want to side with the majority, but truth demands that we stand alone sometimes. Someone spray painted the following slogan on a construction wall on a college campus to show the absurdity of this reasoning: "Be an existentialist—60 billion bugs can't be wrong."

"But Columbus, no one believes the world is round."
"The vast majority of scientists believe in evolution."
"But Dad, everybody is doing it."

The simple question is, "Does that make it right?" When did reality become a democracy? The next time someone says,

"Everybody's doing it," just reply, *"Consensus gentium,"* and wait for a relevant argument.

Argumentum ad Verecundiam (appeal to authority). "Accept this because some authority said it." As we all know, "authorities" can be wrong, and often are. Furthermore, there are conflicting authorities. Which one should I accept? The mere appeal to authority should never be substituted for evidence or a good argument.

However, it is not always wrong to trust an authority. We should trust an authority if we have good reason to believe he is in possession of relevant evidence we don't have. In brief, we trust an authority if he is trustworthy.

No one can know everything. That is why we rely on authorities. That's fine, as long as the authority is trustworthy. But what authorities can we really trust? How can we tell? Here are some guidelines:

1. There must be evidence that one is really an authority before his testimony can be trusted. What is the first question the D.A. always asks an expert witness? "What are your credentials?" Anyone can claim to be an authority, but can he prove it? Our society generally recognizes only two types of credentials: academic and first-hand experience. We believe an economics professor because of the first and we believe a witness of a murder because of the second.

2. Authorities out of their field have no authority. It really doesn't matter how many degrees a person has in nuclear physics, that doesn't mean he knows how to cook. A good example of an authority overstepping his bounds is Isaac Asimov's *Guide to the Bible.* Now, the man certainly is an expert in physics, biochemistry, science fiction, cosmology, and humanism, but he has no authority in writing about the Bible.

3. Legitimate authorities can be trusted because they have the evidence. You trust your doctor because he knows just what the symptoms of pneumonia are. You trust your lawyer because he knows what will stand up before a judge. They not only have the evidence; they know what it means. That type of authority is the kind you can and should appeal to for a sound argument. If someone doesn't have the evidence, he shouldn't open his mouth.

4. Even legitimate authorities may disagree. Just because one authority says something does not mean that all authorities

agree with him. Whenever there is controversy over an issue, the appeal to authority is weakened in direct proportion to the strength of the controversy. Sooner or later we have to appeal to the evidence itself, about which the authorities are arguing. After all, we only asked the authority because he had the evidence.

5. Any appeal to authority is justified if there is evidence that it is an ultimate authority. "This is true because God said it" is an appeal to an ultimate authority, but there must be good evidence that God said it. Remember that Muslims believe the Koran is what God said, Mormons believe the *Book of Mormon* is what God said, and Christian Scientists believe that *Science and Health* is what God said.

The bottom line is this: all appeals to authority ultimately rest on the evidence that the authority has. The only reason to quote an authority is that he knows the evidence better than we do. The letters after his name don't mean a thing without the evidence to back up his position.

Argumentum ab Annis (argument because of age). This fallacy makes the mistake of thinking that all truth is subject to aging. It sets time as an authority, with new ideas being more valuable than old ones. You have heard people say, "This is wrong because it is dated," or "That's an old view." Advertisers love this gimmick because some people will buy anything that says, "New! Improved!" Really, though, it is just chronological snobbery.

> "Belief in God's immutability is based on an outmoded Greek view of substance."
> "Sexual abstinence before marriage is Victorian."
> "The premillennial view is a very recent position."

In each case there is an assumption that truth depends on age. A belief is rejected because it is old or young. But that is beside the point. What is the *evidence* for the position? What *reasoning* supports it? It doesn't matter how many birthdays it's had.

Argumentum ad Futuris (argument to the future). Here is the perfect argument for the eternal optimist: "Accept this because future evidence will support it." It appeals to the authority of Progress with a capital *P*! Face it; this is hope, not proof. It is argument by anticipation, not demonstration. No poker player would dare to pick up the pot because he felt sure he would win the next hand before he got his cards. No logician can do it either.

> "Missing links may yet be found to support evolution."
> "Scientists may soon find a natural cause for the origin of life."
> "Archeology will one day disprove the Bible."

If wishes were fishes, arguments like these could supply a sardine factory. But rational decisions must be based on real evidence, not speculations.

Fallacies of Stacking the Deck

Some people figure that the best way to win an argument is to cheat. So they design their reasoning in such a way that they can't lose. Just like a card player who stacks the deck, some debaters lay out the argument beforehand so that no one else has a chance. There are several ways this can be done.

Petitio Principii (begging the question). This is an argument where the conclusion is sneaked into the premises. It says, "Accept this conclusion as true because the premise from which it comes is true." It is a circular argument, where the conclusion actually becomes a premise. If you start out with the conclusion as the first premise, it really doesn't matter what the second premise is, you can still reach the conclusion you want. We call this "begging the question," because the very question being asked is given the desired answer before any reasoning is done. It is like asking, "Why is the sky blue?" and being told, "Because its blueness makes it look blue." You end up having to beg for an answer.

> The Bible is inspired because 2 Timothy 3:16 says, "All Scripture is inspired by God. . . ."

By referring to the Bible as proof, there is an implicit assumption that the Bible has divine authority. But that is the very question being asked! You can't just say that the Bible says it came from God; so does the Koran. This assumed premise restates the conclusion and begs the question.

Which premise in the following argument guarantees an anti-supernatural conclusion?

A miracle, being by definition an exception to the laws of nature, is based on the lowest degree of probability.
But a wise man should always base his belief on the highest degree of probability.
Therefore, a wise man should never believe in miracles.

(Hint: if I were to roll three dice and get three sixes on the first roll with the odds at 216 to 1 against it, should you believe that it happened?)

Straw man. Another way to stack the deck against the opposition is to draw a false picture of the opposing argument. Then it is easy to say, "This should be rejected because this (exaggerated and distorted) picture of it is wrong." The name of the fallacy comes from the idea that if you set up a straw man, he is easier to knock down than a real man. And that is exactly the way this fallacy works: set 'em up and knock 'em down. It is argument by caricature. It avoids dealing with the real issues by changing the opposition's views.

"Creationists believe that the earth was created in 4004 B.C."
"If men are saved by grace, then they may as well continue to sin so that they can use more grace." [cf. Rom. 6:1ff.]

In both instances, a distorted image of the opposing view is given. Some creationists hold to an old earth, and some who believe in a young earth don't hold to 4004 B.C. The real issue is *that* the earth was created, not *exactly when*. The other objection is dealt with quite well by Paul. These are straw men ready to be hung.

A frequent example of a straw man is this mangling of the cosmological argument:

Everything needs a cause.
God is a thing.
Therefore, God needs a cause.

The problem here is that the law of causality is misstated in the first premise. Theists do not claim that every *thing* needs a cause. The law of causality says that every *event* needs a cause. God is not an event—he is eternal and had no beginning. He is; he doesn't happen. The beginning of the world, on the other hand, is an event and does need a cause.

Special Pleading. This is yet another way to make certain the opposing view doesn't get a fair shake. Here only the evidence that supports one view is cited, and the rest is left out. This is the fallacy of saying, "Accept this because this select evidence supports it (even though other evidence is neglected)." If there are ten studies that show your view to be false, ignore them and make a big point about the one that confirms your conclusion. Really, this argument counts on the listener to be ignorant of the facts. That way anything can be claimed, and no objection can be raised. However, if someone knows about the other ten studies, you're in trouble. This kind of argument can be torn apart easily if all the facts are made known.

"The holocaust proves that there is no God."

But what about the good arguments for the existence of God? What about the Exodus, Hanukkah, and all the daily reminders of his goodness towards all people?

"This survey says that 51% of the people in this country favor abortion."

Why not be honest? There are lots of surveys on this issue, and almost all of them agree that about 57 percent of the country is opposed to abortion on demand and only about 20 percent favor it. You can't just decide that the one you like is the one that is right.

It is easy to stack the deck by giving people only the information that you want them to have, but it is no way to determine truth.

Fallacies of Diversion

The next two fallacies attempt to win the argument by changing the subject. Like a con man running a shell game, they hope that you will be distracted enough not to notice that they have diverted attention away from anything resembling the issues and have focused in on something else. If your opponent is really good at this, he will probably bring up an issue that is highly emotional and unsolvable. The strict logician may be stuck looking for the pea that used to be the subject of discussion only to find that his counterpart has conveniently palmed it and thrown it away.

Ignoratio Elenchi (irrelevant conclusion). This is the more subtle of the two tactics, but the effect is the same. An irrelevant conclusion gets the focus off of the point to be proved by substituting a related, but logically irrelevant, point for it. "Accept this because a loosely associated (but irrelevant) premise is true." The two subjects are similar, but proving one does not say anything about the other. This type of argument is a kind of positive guilt by association. It changes the subject by proving a different conclusion (an irrelevant one) from the one that needs to be proven.

"Reincarnation is true because past-life regression answers a lot of questions and helps people make sense out of their lives."

The two questions here are loosely related, but proving one does not guarantee that the other is true. The results of regression therapy may be totally unrelated to the truth of reincarnation. It might work for any number of reasons (maybe it helps people to have an explanation even if it is not true), and there is no way to tell how well it will work in the long run. It is possible that past-life regression is nothing more than creative imagining or the power of suggestion. What happens in a psychiatrist's office tells us nothing about what happens in the afterlife. This is a ploy to change the subject.

We might mention that this same error is used in numerous contexts. It has reached such epidemic proportions that we could give it a fallacy classification of its own: *Operat ergo veritat:* "It works, therefore it is true." Really, this is simply an *ignoratio elenchi.* Results are never a guarantee of truth. Whether something works and whether it is true are two very different issues. Our pragmatism has fooled us into thinking they are identical.

Anytime someone says, "Whatever works for you," or "Try Jesus 'cause it works," he has committed a fallacy. Christianity is true, regardless of what works, and the propositions that support its truth are not based on personal testimonies. (What does it mean for Christianity to "work" anyway? Does it means being persecuted for your faith, dying to self, and losing all possessions, family and home for Christ's sake? That is what he promised.) Virtually all fraudulent products will start off by showing you personal testimonies with at least one person saying, "It works." Results don't mean a thing; it's truth that counts.

Red Herring (diverting the issue). The second device for changing the subject is less sneaky; it just does it! Pulling a red herring across the platform will divert attention. So will telling an irrelevant joke. A red herring argument says, "Accept this because this other subject is interesting (funny, witty, etc.)." Rather than proving the point, this fallacy simply evades the question by changing the subject, then proceeding as if the point had been made. Often the other topic bears a superficial resemblance to the one being discussed. Don't let that fool you! If no proof is given, there is no reason to accept the argument. One common red herring is to tell a joke to get off the hot seat.

1. "He must be a genius; he certainly is no fool."
2. Reporter: "Senator, will you continue your campaign now that the polls show you far behind?"
   Candidate: "I don't believe in polls."
3. Response to gospel: "I *am* doing what God says: `Eat, drink, and be merry, for tomorrow we die.'"

Fallacies of Generalization

Several fallacies come from trying to make everything fit into one or two categories. The following *faux pauxes* are examples of how we can be made to think everything is black and white if we will just ignore all those other colors. If we dismiss all differences, then everything is the same. Usually though, differences are at least as important as similarities, and in logic they are more important. While such simplifications seem to clarify the issues, they do so at the expense of sometimes crucial distinctions.

Dicto Simpliciter (fallacy of the general rule). This fallacy applies a general rule to a particular case that has significant differences from the general cases to which the rule properly applies. The logic used here says, "Accept this in this case (with special circumstances) because it is true in general." The problem, of course, is that the special circumstances might be just the ones that nullify the rule. One logic text calls this the fallacy of accident, because accidental circumstances render the rule inapplicable. A common example of this is to take the general rules about life given in the Bible and use them as commands that apply to all situations. "A wise son [accepts his] father's discipline" (Prov. 13:1) does not apply to the son whose father comes home drunk and beats him. But one of the best examples is the second temptation of Christ (Matt. 4:6). Satan said:

> "If you are the Son of God throw Yourself down; for it is written, `He will give His angels charge concerning You'; and `On their hands they will bear You up, lest You strike Your foot against a stone.'"

This was a general rule given in the Psalms for the confidence of the Lord's anointed (Ps. 91:11–12). However, Jesus responds by citing a more basic principle that explained why Satan's suggestion was not applicable in this case: "On the other hand, it is written, `You shall not put the Lord your God to the test'" (Matt. 4:7). There is a big difference between facing danger with confidence in the Lord and looking for trouble to see if God will bail you out.

Hasty Generalization. "Accept this general conclusion because these (unusual or atypical) cases support it." This is like the general rule fallacy in reverse. It makes general or absolute rules out of common but not unvarying occurrences. It confuses typical and atypical evidence, or ignores atypical evidence entirely, then jumps to a conclusion. It concludes too much from too little, choosing only the evidence it wants (like special pleading). In short, it tries to make the abnormal seem normal, or the merely normal absolute.

> "If Paul recommended wine for Timothy, then it is good for Christians today."

That wine was recommended for *medicinal* use does not mean it was approved for *social* use. The water-diluted wine they drank was not quite a scotch on the rocks, either. There are some serious differences that are wiped out by generalization.

> "Since all religions offer the same kind of miracles to show that they are true, no claim of miracles really provides proof for any religion."

David Hume used this argument to show that even if miracles were possible, they would be meaningless. However, Hume makes a hasty generalization by saying that all miracles are alike. Jesus' miracles of prophetic fulfillment, raising the dead, and his resurrection are quite different from those alleged to confirm other religions. The uniqueness of these miracles speaks loudly to support Christ's claims to be God. In fact, if all other miraculous claims are self-cancelling, then any unique miracles should be accepted as authentic proof for the religion they confirm.

Cliche. Like general rules, cliches may fit perfectly sometimes, but they tend to overgeneralize. Accordingly, they suffer from the same type of abuse in logic. Cliche reasoning says, "Accept this because it accords with a popular maxim." Is that what cliches are for—to provide supporting evidence in a logical argument? This fallacy has been called "maxim mongering."

Not only do cliches suffer from oversimplification, but sometimes they also contradict each other. "Nothing ventured; nothing gained" and "Better safe than sorry" convey two opposite messages. While these sayings make good descriptions of established truth, they provide no evidence to support a conclusion.

> "The Bible must err, because `to err is human' and the Bible was written by humans."

Does this cliche really describe the situation that gave us the Bible? It seems to ignore the divine role in the production of Scripture (2 Tim. 3:16; 2 Pet. 1:21) and the fact that humans don't necessarily err all the time. If the shoe doesn't fit, don't wear it.

Reductive Fallacies

Some fallacies attempt to make a complex issue look simple by considering only one aspect of it. These are called reductive fallacies because they reduce a many-faceted question to a single point. They argue, "Don't accept this, because one of its many complex aspects is to be rejected." It assumes that descriptions on one level exclude or invalidate descriptions on another level. For example, describing a man as a bundle of molecules does not eliminate his description as a body with a soul. In reducing the complex to the simple, difficult questions seem to be easier to understand; however, the simplification process results in a misunderstanding because only a caricature of the issue is presented.

One of the most widely followed arguments against viewing the Bible historically commits this fallacy:

Myths are by nature *more than* objective truths; they are transcendent truths of faith.
But what is not objective is not part of the space-time world.
Therefore, myths (like stories about Jesus and his miracles) are not part of the space-time world.

The argument makes a critical mistake in the second premise by assuming that what is *more than* objective has *no* objective reality. It reduces the complex issue of where the historical facts end and the religious message begins to a simple question of either history or religion. But describing the stories as transcendent truths does not rule out the historical basis and demonstration of those truths. The question cannot be simplified without distorting the whole picture.

Nothing-Buttery. One of the basic reductive fallacies has been called the fallacy of "nothing-buttery," since it argues that something is nothing but some aspect of it. Materialistic philosophers argue that "Man is nothing but matter in motion." Of course, human beings are matter in motion, but this does not mean that they are not more than this. Similarly, some insist that "The mind is nothing but the brain." They claim "Thought is merely chemical action." The problem with all these reductive fallacies is that these "nothing-but" statements imply a "more-than" knowledge. How could I know that I was nothing but my body unless I was more than my body?

Genetic Fallacy. This is a special type of reductive fallacy in which the single issue focused on is the source or origin of an idea. The argument demands, "Something (or someone) should be rejected because it (or he) comes from a bad source." This is an attempt to belittle a position by pointing out its inauspicious beginnings. "Can any good thing come out of Nazareth?" One form of this is refutation by psychoanalysis. It searches the secrets of the past for hidden motives to determine whether a proposition has any truth to it. By this criterion, we should not believe our model for the benzene molecule because its founder based it on a dream of a snake biting its tail.

One prominent use of this objection in recent years has been to criticize creationism as a scientific view because it comes from

Genesis, a religious source. But that is completely irrelevant. Creation science is a theory that must be evaluated on its own merits and cannot be ruled out simply because it comes from a religious source. So does the idea that murder is wrong, but no one is taking that to the Supreme Court.

Complex Question. "When did you stop beating your wife?" That is a perfect example of asking a complex question. It isn't really one question; it is two. If only one response is given, no matter which question it answers, the other question has an implied answer that may not be true. The debater here is saying, "Accept this (false) implication because of this other (true) implication." It assumes a simple yes-*or*-no answer to a complex yes-*and*-no question. In this respect it is the opposite of a reductive fallacy because it unnecessarily complicates the question. Besides that, at least one of the questions is based on a false assumption. It is the false assumption that usually sticks in the listeners' minds and wins them over to the false proposition.

"Do you believe the world was created in six days, as the Bible says?"

On the surface that sounds like a straightforward question. However, there are people who believe that God created the world, as the Bible says, but not in six consecutive twenty-four-hour periods. They interpret the days to be either long periods of time or single bursts of creating with long intervals of equilibrium in between. How are they supposed to answer that question? "Yes" indicates that they accept the consecutive-day view and "No" implies that they believe in evolution.

Category Mistake. Another fallacy based on confusion is the category mistake. This is an "apple-and-oranges" error because it mixes up two ideas that don't belong together. It says, "Accept this (apple) because it falls into that (orange) category." What kinds of things get confused? Just about anything. But a good example might be the categories of color and taste: "What does blue taste like?" As you can tell, this is a meaningless question, because colors don't have taste. This kind of mistake happens often in questions about God, because he is often in a category all by himself.

"Who were Adam's parents?"
"Who made God?"

"What caused Lucifer to sin?"

"What happened the moment before time began?"

In each of these cases, there is a mistake of asking, "What came before the first?" or "What caused the first cause?" If it is first, then nothing came before. The category `before' does not apply to the category `first.' It is logically impossible. God is the first cause of all things; he is eternal and uncreated. Adam and Eve were the first parents. Lucifer caused his own sin by his own will; nothing outside of him made him do it. There was no moment before time began; there was no time before the first moment of time. There was just eternity.

Faulty Analogy. The technique of arguing by analogy has produced some very convincing arguments. However, not all analogies are created equal. Some simply aren't as relevant as they claim to be because of a critical difference in the things compared. Remember, as long as you ignore the differences, everything is the same. This fallacy deals with the misuse of analogies in logical argument. One who commits this error is saying, "Accept this because of these (superficial) similarities with that." As we said, sometimes analogies can be used to present very strong and effective arguments, but analogies are good only when there are strong similarities and only nonessential differences between the things being compared. But if the similarities are only accidental or the differences are essential, then the argument suffers and can be accused of this fallacy. Likewise, if some similarities are found but there is an essential difference in the aspect being compared, the analogy can be invalidated.

"Believing in Jesus is like believing in the tooth fairy."

When was the last time you saw a book devoted to the historical evidence for the existence and claims of the tooth fairy? How many Ph.D.s devote their lives to studying the tooth fairy's life? The only similarity in this analogy is that the word *believe* is used for both.

"When men repent, they make a real change, so when the Bible says that God repents, that means he must change too."

Is it right to assume that God is like men in all respects? It is always possible that the Bible sometimes uses language that men can relate to even if it isn't theologically precise (like when it says that God has hands, wings, loins, etc.). If God is immutable (unchanging), why would we think that this suggestion of change should be understood without metaphor?

Argument of the Beard. "Reject this because it differs only in degree from what you already reject." The key word is *degree.* The name of the fallacy comes from the question, "When does a man have a beard?" The answer is hard because there is no clear line between not shaving for a few days and having a beard. It is a matter of degree. This fallacy offers a comparison between the view that we hold and a view that we rightly reject, but like a faulty analogy, it assumes that adding up small differences does not make a big difference. It tells us that if a line is hard to draw, then it is impossible to draw. Again, this ignores important distinctions that should be made.

> "Since everyone is more or less good and evil, and all are sinners before God, we should not call Hitler evil and Mother Teresa good."

This thinking says that all degrees of good are lost, with the result that there is no difference between good and evil. Since we reject any absolute goodness in men, we are told to reject any relative goodness too. This blurring of distinctions sounds logical to some degree, but something instinctively tells us there is a real difference between Charles Manson and Abraham Lincoln.

Other Types of Fallacies

Faulty Dilemma. One of the favorite ways to make a Christian squirm is to give him a dilemma that forces him to reject the truth of Christianity. However, most of the dilemmas used are subject to this fallacy. Here the opponent forces one into an either/or answer when the question has a third alternative. He says, "Accept this or that, both of which are contrary to your position," but doesn't mention a third alternative. The key to avoiding the dilemma is simply to find the third alternative. Here are some rather famous dilemmas.

> "Rabbi, who sinned, this man or his parents, that he should be born blind?" [cf. John 9:2–3]

Jesus' response to this question shows that there is a third alternative to this either/or question: "[It was] neither [that] this man sinned, nor his parents; but [it was] in order that the works of God might be displayed in him." In other words, he was born blind so that Jesus could heal him and give the people a chance to believe. This alternative was left out of the thinking that all suffering is a result of sin.

The plague is a punishment from God.
If the priest fights the plague, he is fighting against God.
If the priest does not fight the plague, he is being cruel and inhumane.
So, either the priest fights against God, or he is cruel and inhumane.

Albert Camus constructs this dilemma in his novel *The Plague*. But has he exhausted all the possibilities for the priest's actions? A third explanation might be that since man is responsible for bringing evil into the world (the plague), then he need not worry about fighting against God while trying to remove the effects of evil. Hence, the priest can fight the plague and still serve God by doing good in the evil circumstances. It is not an either/or, but a both/and situation.

Everything happens either by determinism or by free will.
If all is determined, we are wrong to talk about free choices (e.g., to sin, to accept Christ, etc.).
If there is free will, we are wrong to say that God is in control of all things.
Therefore, either we are wrong about free will or we are wrong about God's control.

This kind of argument goes on even between Christians! The debate has produced a great deal of heat and very little light. The problem is that there is a false dilemma set up in the first premise. Determinism and free will are not necessarily contradictory; it is possible that both are true. For centuries, pagan and Christian philosophers alike have offered a simple solution to the dilemma by adding a third alternative. That answer is that God determined that a choice will be freely made. In other words, it is possible for God to use free will as a means to do what has been determined. This does not inhibit freedom either experientially (because the person does not know what choice is determined and feels that the choice is his) or really (because there is no coercion or force involved). This is no dilemma if this third path is taken, because the opposition of free choice and determinism is eliminated. Both God's sovereignty and man's responsibility can be maintained.

Hypothesis Contrary to Fact. Have you ever found yourself wondering what it would be like if you had made different choices in your life? Playing "What if?" games seems fun at first, but inevitably one realizes that there are too many other variables that would change and you *really don't know* how things in the present might have turned out.

This is the same problem that people using this fallacy face. They insist, "Accept this because it might have been this other way." Playing "What if?" games doesn't work in logic any better than it does in real life. It is easy to say, "Things would be different if this other hypothesis were true," but the fact is that *the other hypothesis is not true!* If it were true, we would be living in a different reality—another world; however, our argument is about the way things are in *this* world. Sure it would be different if there were no such thing as gravity, but gravity is a fact that we have to deal with in this world, and no amount of "What if?" can change it. One is asked to assume what might have been to prove what is. This is an "if wishes were fishes" argument. It is based on fantasy, not fact.

> "If Adam had never sinned, Christ would not have needed to die."
> "If Jesus had not been resurrected, then we could not be saved."
> "If we could only remember our past lives, then we would all realize that we are eternal, divine beings."

The problem with each of these arguments is that we can't get beyond that "If." There is no guarantee that reality would be as the statements say, even if their hypotheses were true. We just don't know. Sound reasoning is built, as Joe Friday said, on "Just the facts, Ma'am."

Prestige Jargon Fallacy. Another type of logical snobbery is to say things in such a complex way that people don't dare to question the truthfulness of what has been said. How can they? First, they have to figure out what it means! This is the prestige jargon fallacy (which is a fancy way of saying "fancy talk"). It confuses complexity with authenticity. It attempts to gain credibility through profundity and substitutes technical terminology for truth.

> Karl Marx: Capital is "that dead labor that, vampire like, only lives by sucking living labor, and lives the more the more labor it sucks."
>
> Post-tribulationist: "Pre-tribs have rapture fever generated by an eschatological cancer that eats the vitals from Christian involvement in the present world and is born of an escapist mentality."

Slippery Slope Fallacy. This is the kind of reasoning that says, "Reject this because it will slip into that." It is a domino-theory type of argument that insists that one proposition (which might be accepted in itself) should be rejected because it will lead to a different proposition that is unacceptable. In some instances, such a claim might be true, but it is a fallacy when the connection between the two statements is not *logical*, but *psychological* (or sociological, or historical, etc.). In other words, some statements lead us to other conclusions by logical necessity (that is what this book is all about), but other statements have only sentimental connections with one another. It is a logical fallacy to assert that the connection is necessary, or at least inevitable.

Suppose someone says, "If we feed the Russians, we will have to fight them." There is an intuitive connection between these statements that such a possibility exists; but what is the logical connection between "feeding" and "fighting"? Without a real logical connection, there is no slippery slope to slide down and no series of dominoes to fall.

There is at least one notable argument that avoids this fallacy. In this case, a logical connection can be found.

> "If you can't trust someone (or some book) that claims to be infallible in everything it says, then you can't trust it in anything."

The Bible claims to be infallible (John 10:35; 17:17; Prov. 30:5–6). But today many people are saying that the Bible should be trusted only in religious matters, not in scientific and historical areas. However, the Bible claims to be completely without error, even to the smallest parts of words (Matt. 5:17–18; Gal. 3:16). If this is so, then either we can trust the Bible in all that is says, or we can trust it in nothing. If it did not make the claim to be infallible, it would be a different story; but that gets us back to Hypothesis Contrary to Fact. If the Bible says that it is inerrant, but has errors, then we have no idea where those errors are and we have no reason to trust any part of it. If Jesus claimed to tell the truth in all things, but lied or was mistaken about some, then we have no reason to believe anything that he said. Errors would prove that he was not speaking as God's spokesman, and he might be wrong at any time. The very claim to authority itself is wrong, so how can anything else be trusted? This slippery-slope argument is valid because a logical connection does exist between the propositions. (If the premise, "All parts of the Bible are inerrant," is false, its subaltern, "Some parts of the Bible are inerrant," is undetermined. Hence, inerrancy cannot be affirmed for any single part of the Bible.) The claim to divine authority for all is invalidated if it is invalid for any.

By the same token, Mary Baker Eddy, who claimed to be speaking infallible truth that her God was dictating to her, can be discredited by showing a single error in the things that she wrote. If this argument can discredit all of Scripture, it can also discredit her writings.

Fallacy of Composition. Some arguments assume that what is true of the parts (or the elements) must also be true of the whole (or group).

> "The all-star team must be better than the regional champions because it is made up of better players."
> "I don't need to see Buchart Gardens, it's just a lot of flowers."

In the first instance, the whole will probably be found to be considerably less than the sum of its parts. In the second, the whole turns out to be more. Knowing what something is made of doesn't mean knowing how the parts fit together. There is not a single part on a car that will run by itself, but it runs great when you put them all together.

Exception. Sometimes the whole does have the characteristics of the parts (for example, if each shingle on a roof is brown, then the whole roof is brown). In these cases the very nature of the characteristic demands that if the part has it, then the whole must also possess it. Hence, if all the parts of the universe are finite and created, then the whole must be finite and created. There is no fallacy here.

Fallacy of Division. Some arguments assume that what is true of the whole is true of the parts.

"Since being is eternal, I must be eternal too."

Here we have the fallacy of composition in reverse. This is a favorite New Age argument (though it has been around since at least the sixth century B.C.), but it wrongly assumes that all being is the same. "Being" here means the abstract category of all things. The Christian response is that some beings are dependent and finite. God's being is eternal, but there are finite beings that depend on God. Just because some being (i.e., God) is eternal, it does not follow that all beings are eternal. The part does not necessarily have all the attributes of the whole. A car may be able to go sixty miles an hour. But the carburator by itself will not sustain that speed, no matter how hard I throw it.

There is No End

Of making many fallacies there is no end. For every right way to think there is at least one wrong way. The real shocker is that the wrong ways often sound more persuasive! This is the power of sophism. So as not to be trapped in the persuasive pit of these fallacies, practice in recognizing them is necessary. Take a look at some of these puzzlers!

Exercises for Chapter 6

Determine which fallacy is being committed in the following exercises. There may be more than one fallacy present for each example.

1. Either God exists or evil exists, you can't have both.
2. There is no scientific proof for creation, therefore evolution must be true.
3. All Christians are hypocrites, just look at Jim Bakker.
4. Where did God come from?

5. Most scholars reject the natural arguments for God's existence.

6. I am firm in my belief that if you weren't so pig-headedly stubborn, you would see the truth of Christianity.

7. Your worldview suffers from axiomatic complications that render it truth-functionally incoherent.

8. What's wrong with TM? It reduces stress, helps concentration, and is very relaxing.

9. You are defending the existence of God because you already believe in him, not because you are searching for truth.

10. Natural arguments for God's existence are something that they did during the Middle Ages when they had nothing better to do. Today what's important is living a meaningful religious life.

11. If a person gives up belief in the inerrancy of the Bible, it won't be long before he stops believing in God.

12. Some say that our belief in Christ's second coming is just sensationalism. Well, I think the Bible is a pretty sensational book.

13. I know philosophers are intelligent people because if they weren't intelligent, they wouldn't be philosophers.

14. The Declaration of Independence guarantees me the right to life, liberty, and the pursuit of happiness. Having this baby would deny me those rights, therefore I am justified in having an abortion.

15. My biology professor says there is no God, and he's a scientist, so he would know.

16. We should not feel bothered if we offend people with the gospel. After all, in order to make an omelette you have to break a few eggs.

17. Have you stopped cheating on exams?

18. You can't trust anything he says. He's an atheist and has no basis for morality.

19. You Christians believe you are the only ones who have the truth.

20. Salvation can't be a free gift. As the old saying goes, "You get what you pay for."

21. Atheistic philosophers have made some good points, so atheism is a legitimate world view.

22. You'd better believe that Christianity is true or else you'll go to hell!

23. Nobody believes that Adam-and-Eve story anymore.
24. We Christians must choose. We either break the law and block the doors of abortion clinics, or we take the guilt of the death of these unborn babies on ourselves.
25. All philosophers have some truth and some good arguments, and none of them are completely right. I guess you have to be a skeptic and not take any view.
26. I know that every action we perform is predetermined because no one has proved we have free will.
27. TV can't be harmful to children, because it occupies their attention and keeps them off the streets.
28. I believe that everyone will go to heaven because God understands that we aren't perfect, but we try hard to be good.
29. Aristotle said in his *Nichomachean Ethics* that the `good' is whatever a good man approves of, and you can tell a good man because he always approves of the good.
30. Where was the man when he jumped off the bridge?
31. If you study theology you will become so rationalistic that you will lose your first love for God. Your heart for God will become pure head knowledge.
32. Kant disproved the ontological argument, therefore none of these rational arguments are accepted anymore.
33. Most Americans are pro-choice.
34. The terms we used to discuss concepts like `soul' and `mind' are archaic and outdated. Neurophysiology is on the verge of finding new physicalistic ways of describing how our mind relates to our bodies. In the future we will be able to do away with the `soul'.
35. Our pastor told us that evolution couldn't possibly be true.
36. I will not commit that act because it is unjust. I know it is unjust because my conscience tells me so, and my conscience tells me so because the act is wrong.
37. Leibniz contends that this world is the best of all possible worlds that God could have made. What a ridiculous assertion! Everything in this world is not as good as it could be.
38. It is wrong to go to war because the Bible says, "Thou shalt not kill."
39. Do you believe the Bible is true when it teaches that women are inferior to men?

40. All of the manuscripts of the Bible have variations, so this one can't be trusted.
41. Telling Christians that salvation is free and that they just need to believe is like signing a contract to buy a house and never making any of the house payments.
42. Advertisement: Just Received! A new stock of shirts for men with 15 to 19 necks.
43. We should question the Newtonian worldview because he believed that God created the universe and that surely affected his view of things.
44. If the church hadn't had such a grip on the people during the Middle Ages, Christianity would have died out before the Renaissance.
45. Most atheists reach a point in their lives where they reject God because of a personal crisis, so their arguments can't be taken seriously.
46. Most people believe in God, and they can't all be wrong.
47. I don't think we should ask people about their private religious beliefs because we might offend them and it's better to be safe than sorry.

7

Uncovering Logic in Literature

By now you have a fairly good grasp of how to analyze a syllogism to determine its form and validity. But there is one more question we have to ask about a syllogism: Would you know one if it bit you? If you were reading the newspaper and the editorialist committed a four-term fallacy, would you be able to see it?

The problem with knowing logical form and function is that only logicians spell out their arguments in syllogisms. Everyone else just seems to ramble on. But does that mean that people don't use syllogistic arguments? Of course they do! We just have to transpose their thinking from literary form to logical form. You probably will be surprised by just how often standard syllogisms are used in the things you read every day. In this chapter we will talk about four steps in converting arguments from literature into logic; then we will get some practice at it.

First, Find the Conclusion

It seems like a backward way of going about it, but it is always best to find the conclusion first, then look for the rest of the argument. After all, we are not *building* a syllogism, we are taking it apart. The piece that is put on last is the first one to be taken off. Besides, if we know the conclusion, then we can identify two of the three terms—the subject and predicate terms are the subject and predicate of the conclusion. The only one we won't know then is the middle term. By starting with the conclusion, we know where the author is going; we just have to find out how he got there.

How do you find the conclusion? First, look for some key words like *therefore, hence, then, thus, so, so that,* etc. Sometimes the writer makes it easy and says, *"In conclusion."* All of these are ways of drawing your attention to the point he wants to make. Any time you see a *therefore,* you really ought to find out what it's there for.

In addition to these key words, the conclusion is usually stated either first or last in the unit you are dealing with. Since it is the main point, writers will either state it and then support it, or lead you down a road toward it. Unless the matter is really poorly written, you should be able to figure out the main point the author is trying to make, and it is generally safe to consider that his conclusion.

By the way, there is one more reason to find the conclusion first. There may be a fallacy in the argument you are studying, and it is easier to see where a mistake was made if you know what the author was trying to accomplish. If you tried to find the premises first, you might never find the conclusion, because it might not follow from the premises stated. Knowing the conclusion at least gives you an idea of how the author thought his terms were related, even if he was wrong.

Find the conclusion in the following examples:

> Indeed, if the faith is based on infallible truth and it is impossible for what is contrary to truth to be demonstrated, then it is clear that arguments advanced against the faith are not demonstrative and can be disproven. [Aquinas, *Summa Theologica,* I, 1.8]

> And she had never forgotten that, if you drink much from a bottle marked "poison," it is almost certain to disagree with you, sooner or later. However, this bottle was *not* marked "poison," so Alice ventured to taste it, and, finding it very nice . . . she very soon finished it off.[1]

You might remember that the result of drinking this bottle was that Alice found herself to be only seven inches high. Where did she go wrong? A classic case of disastrously denying the antecedent!

1. Lewis Carroll, *Alice's Adventures in Wonderland* (New York: New American Library, 1960), p. 22

Reconstruct the Sentences

Once you have found the conclusion, you are ready to begin reconstructing the other premises. That is, they must be converted from literary to logical form. Logical form is *S is P* or *S is not P*. It is usually helpful to spell this out in words: "S is in the category of P." Even draw circles; they will help you visualize the logic (see Chapter 3).

The reason for spelling things out like this is obvious from the following example. Often you will run into statements with no verb "is" or "is not." In their normal literary form, these sentences have the logical subject at the end and the predicate at the beginning. Unless they are translated into their proper logical form, you will not know which terms are distributed and which are not. And without knowing distribution, you cannot know if they are valid. Consider this sentence:

Literary form: Sin characterizes all human beings.
Logical form: All human beings are (in the category of) sinful beings.

Just looking at the literary form, you might mistakenly think that *Sin* was the subject of the proposition, when actually it is "all human beings."

Once you know the conclusion and spell it out in logical form, then you can do the same for the premises. That may seem like a lot of work to begin with, but there are no short-cuts to clear, logical thinking. So find the conclusion and then follow these steps:

First, identify the subject of your conclusion. That subject has to be either the subject or predicate of the minor premise. Now do you see that term anywhere else in the argument? Congratulations, you have just located the minor premise. Now, for the major premise, do the same thing with the predicate of the conclusion. The predicate of the conclusion is always either the subject or predicate of the major premise. You really can't miss. Whatever premise the subject of the conclusion is mentioned in must be the minor premise. And whatever premise the predicate of the conclusion is stated in must be the major premise.

There are two things that may make this process harder than it ought to be. For example, what if you have looked every-

where and the author never used those words again in his
whole lifetime? Then, you have to remember what your eighth-
grade creative writing teacher kept trying to drill into your head,
"Good writing isn't repetitive. Good writers find interesting
ways to say the same things." Even though the exact words are
not there, the idea might still be there in a different form. It
might even be stated positively in the conclusion but negatively
in the premise.

Sometimes you have to go with a general idea that is the
same, even if none of the words look alike. Don't let poetic
license throw you off the course of finding the logic.

But what if there is just no mention of the term at all? Then
you need to remember that syllogisms can take alternate forms
like the enthymeme, where one or more premises may be
implied, but not stated. In that case, you need to figure out what
premise is needed to get to the conclusion from wherever you
are. This can be tricky if the conclusion is the missing premise,
but it's not usually impossible. If the content of the missing
premise were not pretty obvious, then the writer would not
have left it out.

When you are searching for the premises and reconstructing
the syllogism, it is helpful to look for key words like, *for, since, in
view of,* and *because.* These words tell you that an explanation is
about to be given. They introduce the reasoning that a premise
provides. They imply a necessary logical relationship. Sometimes
the point they explain is a proof of one of the premises, rather
than stating the premise itself. On other occasions, a whole list
of *for*s may introduce a list of individual pieces of evidence that
build up an inductive argument rather than a deductive one.
These are the kind of words that tell you how everything in the
passage relates to the whole. Finding them helps you see which
sentences explain the conclusion you have found. Try to reconstruct the arguments of both sides in this interchange from Peter
Kreeft's book, *Socrates Meets Jesus.*

> Bertha Broadmind: But if your god is unchanging, you live in a
> static world. There's no possibility of progress.
> Socrates: Exactly the opposite, I think. . . . Would you not
> define progress as change for the better?
> Bertha: Yes.
> Socrates: And better means closer to the best?
> Bertha: Yes.

Socrates: And the god is the best. . . .

Bertha: So?

Socrates: Suppose the god, the goal of progress, is changing. Then progress becomes impossible. How could we progress toward a goal that keeps receding? How could a runner make progress toward a finish line if someone kept moving it as he ran?

Bertha: He couldn't.

Socrates: Then if the god progresses, you cannot progress, for the god is your goal. Without an unchanging goal you cannot judge any change as progress.[2]

Look for the Middle Term

Now that you have the conclusion and the premises, the next step is easy. In fact, you already have the middle term in the premises that you reconstructed. Now you just have to identify it. It is not too hard to find because it is the only term that occurs twice in the premises but is not in the conclusion.

If you have already found the major and minor premises, then the part that was not in the conclusion is the middle term. Also, the middle term is always the pivotal term on which the whole argument turns. As you read through a passage, you will notice that your thinking moves away from the major premise to the minor premise. The point at which that happens is about where you will find the middle term. It specifies the relationship between the major and minor terms, then quietly gets out of the way.

Identify the middle term here:

Chico: We gotta catch-a these guys. How we gonna do it?

Harpo: (displays a piece of fly paper)

Chico: No, that's-a no good. Baseball players catch flys; these guys are foot-a-ball players.

[The Marx Brothers, *Horsefeathers*]

All right, the logic is a little mixed up here (that is what comedy is all about), but there is a definite middle term that makes the joke work. In fact, what makes it funny is the equivocation on that middle term. But the best way to kill a joke is to explain it.

2. Peter Kreeft, *Socrates Meets Jesus* (Downers Grove, Ill.: InterVarsity Press, 1987), 30–31.

State Each Premise in Logical Form

You have found everything that can be found in the passage. Now what do you do with it? Try to put it into the form in which it is easiest to work with—simple logical form. This step can be really tricky, because there is no telling what a writer might do to make his simple logic "interesting." It may seem like there is no way to translate a mile-long string of subordinate clauses into a Type A, E, I, or O sentence, but, like trying to figure out how a magic trick was done, you have to remember that it is a trick, and keep remembering that until you work it out. Here are some things to watch for.

Look for Equivalent Terms

We mentioned before that a single term can be stated in any number of ways. Before you can put the syllogism into logical form, though, you have to find one way to state it that will fit all of its uses. This helps you to see through the fog of literary style and keeps you from committing a four-term fallacy. Just look at how many ways this author found to say "pork":

> Although traditional Jewish practices forbid eating the meat of a pig, a large minority of Jews in Israel have developed a taste for bacon, pork, and the rest. This offended Orthodox Jews, who wanted to pass a law prohibiting the sale of these forbidden products. Explained . . . a leader of the Orthodox Jews: ["We don't want to stop people from eating sausage. But it hurts every religious man when he passes a shop with a hog in the window."]

Insert or Convert All Quantifiers

Rarely will you see logical quantifiers written in literature. In fact, most writers find all kinds of tricky ways to avoid using such straightforward talk. It is your job to make sure that all of the *All*s, *No*s, and *Some*s are in the right places so that you can put the argument in logical form. In some cases, that just means inserting a quantifier where it has been omitted. More often, though, you will have to determine which quantifier is meant by the phrase used. For instance, "not all" really means, "some."

Watch out for a phrase like "none but" or "only." In these cases, you have to change the quantifier *only* to *all* and then *reverse the order of the terms*. A simple example is:

Only Triangles have three sides.
becomes
All three-sided figures are triangles.

So you can change the "only" to an "all" and reverse the order of the subject and predicate to get a Type-A premise.

A less obvious example is the sentence "Only fools reject God." We can't just change the quantifier so that it says, "All fools reject God," because that is not true. Let's draw some circles just to be sure.

Figure 7.1

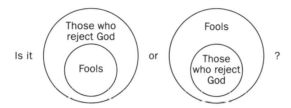

The first set of circles in Figure 7.1 can't be what we want. There are plenty of foolish people who believe in God too. They are just foolish in different ways. It is the second diagram that we are after. So we need to change the order of our terms so that the sentence reads, "All who reject God are fools." This translation for exclusive propositions (where a group is excluded) in which the order of terms must be switched, might be diagrammed as in the circles in Figure 7.2.

Figure 7.2

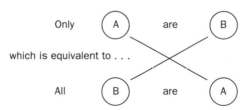

Likewise, sentences with the word *except* require special handling. If the sentence has the phrase *None except*, as in "None except believers will see the kingdom of God," then it is to be treated as an *exclusive sentence* along the order of *only* . . . and *none but.* . . . Thus our example would be correctly translated into: "All who will see the kingdom of God are believers."

However, if the sentence has the phrase *all except*, then that is a horse of a different color. It is not an *exclusive sentence* but an *exceptive sentence*. These are handled differently. Take the example "All except believers in Christ are condemned." This is certainly not the same as "Only believers in Christ are condemned." So, how is it to be translated into standard logical form?

There are actually two options with an exceptive sentence:

1. You can change it to a Type-A proposition and negate the *subject* term: "All who are not believers (or "are non-believers") are condemned." (Note that you can use either "not" or "non-" since it is modifying the subject term and not the copula.) **or**
2. You can make it a Type -E sentence: "No believers are condemned."

Which do you choose? Either will work. However, you should select the one that keeps your syllogism valid and best retains the meaning of the original. In our example, it would probably be best to select number 1, since the original seems to be referring to those who are not believers rather than to those who are, as implied by number 2.

Watch for Conversions of Propositions

One of the poetic devices that writers use is to state things in roundabout ways, like stating positive things negatively and using double negatives. These are however, often the same conversions as the logical conversions that we dealt with in Chapter 3 (conversion, obversion, contraposition, etc.). You need to be aware that a writer may use these as two different ways to say the same thing. For instance, he may say, "The Bible is inerrant" at one point and "No word from God can err" later. This is just the obverse of his original statement. But also, you can use this knowledge to simplify the syllogism that you are constructing. If you read, "Those outside Christian Science do not recognize the prophetic authority of Mrs. Eddy's teachings," it might be easier to see this as the contrapositive of the proposition, "All who recognize Mrs. Eddy's teachings are Christian Scientists." This is just one more tool to make it easier to convert a difficult passage into a simple syllogism.

Some Examples

Now that we have outlined a method for recovering syllogisms from literature, let's try to apply what we know to some familiar passages of Scripture. Who knows, we might even learn something in the process!

> For since the creation of the world His invisible attributes, His eternal power and divine nature, have been clearly seen, being understood through what has been made, so that they are without excuse. [Rom. 1:20]

The first question is, "Where is the conclusion?" Do you see anything to give you a hint? Very good; the *so that* clause does sound like a conclusion. And *for* is a premise. So we have a conclusion and a premise.

All men clearly see God in nature. (premise)
So, all men are without excuse. (conclusion)

From this we know the minor term of the syllogism ("All men") and the major term ("without excuse"). All we need to know now is the middle term. But since that is the term that occurs once in each premise but not in the conclusion, what we need is another premise. In this case the other premise is not stated; it is implied. So we really have an enthymeme. Since the conclusion implies that people are morally responsible for what they see in nature, the missing premise is, "All who see God in nature are without excuse." So the whole argument goes like this:

[All who clearly see God in nature are without excuse.]
All men [are in the category of those who] clearly see God in nature.
So, all men are without excuse.

Next we need to ask, do we have a middle term? By George, we do! "All who clearly see God in nature" is the middle term. It occurs in both premises, but not in the conclusion.

> . . . having become as much better than the angels, as He has inherited a more excellent name than they. For to which of the

angels did He ever say, "Thou art My Son, today I have begotten Thee"? [Heb. 1:4–5]

This passage gives us the conclusion right up front again: Christ is much better than the angels. What premises does the writer use to get that conclusion? The word *For* introduces evidence, but it is in the form of a rhetorical question. The answer expected to this question is "None," and that gives us a place from which to start building. So we have a premise and a conclusion. All we need is another proposition. It is implied in the citation in which God calls Christ his Son. Hence, the premise is, "Christ is called Son by God." So the whole syllogism is:

Whoever is called Son of God is better than angels (who are not).
Christ is called the Son of God.
Therefore, Christ is better than angels.

Now we have all three terms. The subject term of the syllogism is "Christ," which is the subject of the conclusion. The predicate term is "angels," from the predicate of the conclusion. The middle term must be "whoever is called the Son of God," since it alone is mentioned once in each of the premises but not in the conclusion. The syllogism is AAA in figure 1, which—a quick check of the validity chart (in Chapter 3) tells us—is valid. The reason it is valid, though, is because it does not break any of the seven rules of the syllogism (see Chapter 3).

Not all logical arguments are categorical syllogisms, of course. In 2 Peter 2:4–9, we find a series of hypothetical syllogisms. The "If . . . then" structure is retained, but in a way that leads straight to the conclusion. He gives us all of the "If's" first, leaves the affirmation of the antecedent unspoken, and puts all the "then's" together in the conclusion. The result is four similar syllogisms pressed into one compact argument. Peter corrects the false teachers who are saying that there is no judgment with a response that the Pharisees had leveled against the Sadducees and that is recorded in the apocryphal book of Sirach (or Ecclesiasticus) (16:7–9).

For *if* God did not spare angels when they sinned, but cast them into hell and committed them to pits of darkness, reserved for judgment;

and [*if* He] did not spare the ancient world, but preserved Noah, a preacher of righteousness, with seven others, when He brought a flood upon the world of the ungodly;

And [*if*] He condemned the cities of Sodom and Gomorrah to destruction by reducing them to ashes, having made them an example to those who would live ungodly thereafter;

and *if* He rescued righteous Lot, oppressed by the sensual conduct of unprincipled men (for by what he saw and heard [that] righteous man, while living among them, felt his righteous soul tormented day after day with their lawless deeds),

[*then*] the Lord knows how to rescue the godly from temptation, and to keep the unrighteous under punishment for the day of judgment.

The antecedents are stated, but need simplification. The consequents are found in the conclusion. But wait a minute: there are only two consequents for four antecedents! That means that some of the premises will have the same consequents, but not all of them. What's more, when we take a closer look at the passage, we find out that another antecedent has been hidden in the pack. Figure 7.3 shows how it works out:

Figure 7.3

Antecedents		Consequences
If God judged:	angels . . . the ancient world . . . Sodom and Gomorrah . . .	then he knows how to keep the unrighteous for judgment.
If God rescued:	Noah . . . Lot . . .	then he knows how to rescue the godly.

The minor premise is an implied *modus ponens*. (See Chapter 4 if you have forgotten what that means.) Since all of these things are recorded in Scripture, it is true that God did all of these things.

The conclusion then is just a matter of forming a conjunction from the two consequents. That means just putting an *and* between them:

"God knows how to keep the unrighteous for judgment and rescue the godly."

It is not unusual to find arguments combined like this. The force of all of them put together makes a more dramatic effect, and the number of examples adds weight to the evidence. In this case, Noah and Lot being saved from the midst of the destruction heightens the contrast and adds emphasis.

So, that is how it is done. Logic can be found all over the place in literature; you just have to know what to look for. Find the conclusion, reconstruct the premises, identify the middle term, and put the whole argument into logical form. This method for converting prose to logical form may take some practice, but it should work well for you. Now that you can use it to evaluate the deductions that you happen to run across, it is time to move on. There is a whole other field of logic that we have not entered yet. You should be able to handle deductions pretty well by now, so let's try our hands at induction.

Exercises for Chapter 7

In the following exercises, identify the Major term, the Minor term, and the Middle term, or identify the form if other than categorical, for example, *Modus Tollens, Modus Ponens*, etc., and put the arguments in syllogistic form. Finally, tell whether the arguments are formally valid or invalid, and if they are invalid, what fallacy(ies) they commit.

1. Everyone present today is employed at the university. Every member of the organization is present today. So, every member is employed at the university.
2. Bill must be a U.S. citizen because only U.S. citizens are allowed to vote, and Bill has his voter registration card.
3. Only the "A" students are able to achieve success, for only those who have above-average intelligence are able to succeed, and "A" students have above-average intelligence.
4. It is a matter of common knowledge that only those newspapers that print sensational things like murders and illicit love affairs ever attain a wide readership. And decent newspapers do not become involved in this kind of sensationalism. Thus, decent newspapers cannot hope to attain a wide readership.
5. If the God of the Bible were really all-powerful and all-good he would defeat sin. But there is still a lot of sin

going on in this world that isn't yet defeated. But just because sin hasn't been defeated yet doesn't mean it will never be defeated. Consequently, because we know that the God of the Bible is all powerful and that he is all-good, we can be assured that one day he will defeat sin.

6. It is not possible for a thing to be the efficient cause of itself; for so it would be prior to itself, which is impossible. (Thomas Aquinas, *Summa Theologica* I, Question 2, Article 3)

7. It was either Bill who made the final touchdown by receiving a pass, or it was John who scored the final points by leaping over the center for the touchdown. It couldn't have been John because he was taken out of the game just before the final score was made. It must have been Bill who scored the last touchdown.

8. Every news reporter is involved in a certain amount of interpretation of what he reports, since no reporter is able to report every detail of an important event, and the selection of what is important enough to report in the available time involves the act of interpreting the events to identify what is important in the eyes of the reporter.

8

Introduction to Induction

Not all points can be rationally proven. There are some things that can't be decided until we look at the facts. For example, if we ask, "How many Americans believe abortion is wrong?" there is no syllogism that can tell us. We have to ask a whole bunch of Americans in order to find out. Deductive logic has its limits. This is where inductive logic enters the picture. For some things, the only way we can know them is to look at the evidence and evaluate it. But how should that evidence be evaluated? There must be rules for such procedures, and those rules are the principles of inductive logic.

Inductive and deductive logic as such are quite different. In fact, they work backward from each other. Deductive logic can reason from general ideas to particular instances (like from the mortality of men in general to the mortality of John in particular), but inductive logic can reason from particular instances to general conclusions (like from the mortality of Socrates, Aristotle, Moses, Adam, Tom, Dick, and Harry to the mortality of all men).[1] Also, while deductive logic looks at the cause (or condition) and determines what its effect (or consequents) will be, inductive logic observes the effects and tries to find the cause.

Deductive logic is *a priori* reasoning and inductive logic is *a posteriori*. These names come from Latin words meaning that

1. Of course, deductive logic can also reason from universal to universal and inductive can reason from particular to particular. But deductive cannot go from particular to universal, and inductive does not go from universal to particular.

Figure 8.1

Deductive	Inductive
general to particular	particular to general
cause to effect	effect to cause
a priori reasoning	a posteriori reasoning
philosophical reasoning	scientific reasoning
necessary conclusions	probable conclusions

deductive logic draws its conclusions *before*, or prior to, examining experience, but inductive logic draws conclusions only *after* (posterior to) looking to experience.

To our high-tech minds, inductive logic sounds superior, because it is scientific. But there is still a place for the philosophical thinking represented by deduction. After all, once scientific observation provides the premises, we still have to make logical deductions and inferences from them. Today, both philosophers and scientists really use both methods whenever they are needed.

But the biggest difference between deductive and inductive logic is the kinds of conclusions they reach. In deductive logic, the conclusions were either true or false and *had to be that way*. If you built a valid syllogism with true premises and no fallacies, your conclusion must be true. However, induction does not work that way. Here, although the propositions are either true or false, we are not absolutely sure which they are; hence, all conclusions are only probable. They have various degrees of probability from virtual certainty to virtual impossibility, but one can never know absolutely any proposition based on inductive logic. (An exception to this is a "perfect" induction, like "All the coins in my right hand are pennies." If there are only three and we can see and count and identify all three, then we have a perfect induction of which we can be certain.) The reason inductions yield only probable conclusions is that induction is always an argument by analogy. It is an assertion that, because there is a similarity between two things, they will be similar in other respects also. If we were to diagram such an argument, it might look like this:

A, B, C, and D all have qualities p and q.
A, B, and C all have quality r.
Therefore, D has quality r also.

This seems reasonable, as long as there is some connection between qualities p and q and quality r. But can we know that this analogy follows for sure? No, we can't. For example, suppose we choose sparrows, sea gulls, and hummingbirds for A, B, and C above as animals having wings (p) and feathers (q). Now if D is Canadian honkers, then it follows and is true that they do also have quality r, the ability to fly. For almost all birds, this argument works fine. But what if D is the penguin? It has wings and feathers, but it can't fly. Here we see that our conclusion must remain only probable, and we can never claim it to be the absolute truth. The stronger the analogies we draw, though, the more probable our conclusions will be.

The Nature of Probable Conclusions

Because induction is an argument from analogy, extending observations of some to the whole class, it usually involves an *inductive leap*. It requires reaching out beyond what the evidence shows to apply that evidence to other things. It must extend its particular findings to make broad, general statements. This is the case almost all the time, except when we all happen to know all of the particulars. That case is called a perfect induction. Usually, inductive conclusions cannot be called universally true, though, because they are generalizations, and exceptions are always possible. Rather than being true or false, they are more or less probable. They involve *degrees of probability*. Sometimes, these degrees can be measured as to their percentage of accuracy; other times, a percentage can be guessed. This works out fine, because we divide the levels of probability with rather broad strokes. All inductive conclusions should be evaluated for where they stand on this scale. Here is a guideline:

99% ± —Virtually certain: overwhelming evidence in its favor. Things like the law of gravity fit here.

90% ± —Highly probable: very good evidence in its favor. It is highly probable that no two snowflakes will look alike.

70% ± —Probable: sufficient evidence in its favor. Most medicines have to pass this test to be approved.

50% ± —Possible: either no evidence or equipolence of evidence pro and con. The chance that your team will win the coin toss is 50%.

30% ± —Improbable: insufficient evidence in its favor. At this point, no one believes it except the few for whom it worked.

10% ± —Highly improbable: very little evidence in its favor. Like the theory that Jesus spent his early years studying with a Hindu guru.

1% ± —Virtually impossible: almost no evidence in its favor. The existence of unicorns is at this level.

But how can we determine the probability of a conclusion? As we said, sometimes we have real numbers to calculate the probability. We call this *statistical probability*. There are mathematical formulas to help us with this. But when the numbers are not there, we have to weigh the evidence by some other rules. This is known as *empirical probability*. The evidence may be clear, but it doesn't come in the form of hard numbers, so we have to make an intelligent guess at its probability. Let's talk about statistics first, because they are easier.

Figuring Statistical Probability

When figuring the degree of probability for a statistical problem, the first thing we need to do is to make sure that our terms are clearly defined. It does no good to compile a lot of data when the terms you are using are understood by some people in one way and by others in another way. The term *Son of God* has several different meanings for an evangelical, a Jehovah's Witness, a Mormon, and a New Ager. You can't ask them all, "Do you believe Jesus was the Son of God?" and expect to find out what they really believe. Likewise, if you want to know what Methodists believe, you can't assume that the figures for all Christians, or Protestants, or Lutherans will be the same. Define the terms so that you get the information you want.

Also, we must devise sufficient classes to cover all the data. The classes of "Catholic, Protestant, and Jewish" are not sufficient to cover all the data of American religion. These categories leave out Moslems, Hindus, Buddhists, Secular Humanists, and many others. Also, it may not be appropriate to lump all Protestants together for what you are studying, or it might be just as wrong to ignore the factors that unite many Protestants. You have to be sure your results cover all the data you really need.

Make sure you use only one principle of classification. In other words, raise only one question at a time. If the question you want answered is, "When were you baptized?" you can use the principle of age (0–10, 10–20, 20–25, etc.), or relation to church (at birth, at confirmation, after profession of faith, etc.), but don't mix the two. Don't list the options as, "at birth, 15–25, at confirmation, 25–35, etc." This eliminates an answer for children baptized before age fifteen. It also might give two possible answers for those whose age at confirmation is listed. You end up adding apples and oranges and maybe a few tangerines.

This leads us directly to another point: Don't let the classes overlap. If two answers are possible for some people, you will get both from some, neither from others, and still others will answer one or the other without letting you know there is an overlap. These statistics are worthless, because you have no idea which answers give you the information you wanted.

Finally, once all the data are compiled and the numbers are in, you must select the most appropriate method for reporting the results. There are three ways statistics can be stated. The *mean* (average), the *mode* (most frequent), and the *median* (the number halfway between highest and lowest response).

When we talk about averages, we are usually thinking about the *mean*. It can be found by adding together all of the figures and dividing by the number of figures we added. (The mean of 5, 6, 7, 8, and 9 is 7 [35 ÷ 5= 7]). It can be used to find out where the group as a whole stands, like the average score on an examination.

However, there might be no one in the group who actually got that grade on the examination. If you want to find out what most people got, the *mode* is more appropriate. It is found by simply finding what number occurs most often. If the grades were 5, 6, 7, 8, 8, 8, 8, 8, 9, then 8 would be the mode. When we speak of the average man on the street, we probably mean the modal man, or the one we are most likely to run into.

Sometimes, though, what we really need to know is where the middle of the road is for a given question. Then we need to learn the *median* of the group. This is the number that occurs halfway between the highest and lowest numbers in our data, or, in a series consisting of an even number of numbers, a number midway between the two middle numbers. The median of our 5, 6, 7, 8, and 9 series is 7, the same as the mean. The median of the series 2, 4, 8, 12, 16, and 43 is 10 (midway between 8 and 12). Often the median will be close to the mean, but not in cases where there is one piece of data that is much higher or much lower than the other numbers. The median of 1, 2, 3, 50, is 2.5. But since the mean is 14, that may not be the best way to represent the data.

Figuring Empirical Probability

There are four basic questions that must be asked of every inductive argument where empirical data are given. The first is *"How many cases were examined?"* In other words, how broad is the sample? If a survey claims to represent the spectrum of opinions among all Americans, but only twenty people were polled, the conclusion is suspect. The more cases studied, the better the probability that the conclusion is accurate.

The second question is similar to the first: *"How representative is the evidence?"* How much like the real world was the testing environment? In that survey, did all the people polled work in the same office? Or did they represent the spectrum of economic, social, racial, and religious ideas found in this country? The more differences there are between cases, the stronger the conclusion. If the cases studied don't reflect the real world, how can we say the conclusion will hold true for all reality?

A third question that must be asked to determine the degree of probability is *"How carefully was the evidence examined?"* Many queries could be made under the umbrella of this question: How many qualities of similarity were studied? How many differences were studied? Were all possible explanations accounted for? Were the affected results isolated from other causes? Was all the evidence presented? Just how critically was the evidence evaluated? A friend of ours was an assistant in the psychology lab at a major university in his undergraduate days. He frequently saw both graduate students and professors manipulate data to confirm their hypotheses. They would throw out results that didn't fit, experiment without a control group, and redesign the experiment if they didn't get what they expected. Some famous experiments have been widely accepted, but their results have never been reproduced. Among these are tests that indicate that vitamin C helps a cold and the noted Manhattan experiment that showed how aggression increased in a growing colony of rats that has limited space. How do we know that the evidence has really been evaluated critically in such cases? The discipline of comparative religions has long been criticized for stressing the similarities between religions while ignoring the differences. This selective use of evidence lowers the probability of any conclusions.

The fourth and final question is, *How does the information gained relate to the body of knowledge we already have in general?"* Does it contradict anything we are sure of? Or does it help explain things better? Sometimes new evidence can rock the foundations of issues that we thought were settled, but its degree of probability and explanatory usefulness makes it a welcomed discovery. Such was the case with the evidence from the red shift, which destroyed the steady-state theory of the universe. Random radiation had been noted for some time throughout the universe, but only when two scientists sought to find the source of this radiation was it proposed that the entire universe is still giving off the radiation from a huge cosmic explosion that set all things in motion. Many call this the Big Bang. Further studies point to a universe that is still expanding as the shock waves of the explosion go out, although it was expanding faster at one time than it is now. This supports the belief that the universe had a beginning at a definite moment, at a specific time in the past. Scientists who had accepted the wisdom of Einstein, that the universe was always there, were scandalized. They could not believe it. In defending his view, Einstein was finally found to have made a schoolboy error in his mathematics: he had divided by zero. Also, the steady-state theory could only be possible if the universe were always creating hydrogen atoms from nothing, but this has never been seen. The new theory eliminated the need for this speculation, which had no evidence to support it. With this evidence and the way it helped explain things, the old theory has been rejected by most cosmologists.

Kinds of Certainty

Having finished our discussion of degrees of probability, we must raise another question. How certain can we be of probable conclusions? The best way to answer that is to look at the levels of certainty that are available and see where induction rates.

The highest level of certainty is *mathematical certainty*. Numbers don't change; 1 + 1 always = 2, and we can be perfectly certain that this will be the case. Mathematical truths are true by definition. If we understand what the number 1 represents and what adding is, then adding 1 and 1 can't help but make 2. Very close to this is *logical certainty*. We can be logically certain that no contradictions are true. There can be no square circles, because being a circle and having four right angles at the same time in the same sense is impossible. Likewise, tautologies—statements where the predicate defines the subject—have logical certainty. We can be quite sure that all circles are round, that all bachelors are unmarried men, and that the best way to keep a secret is not to tell anybody. These all carry the weight of logical certainty. Furthermore, some statements are *existentially undeniable*. The statement *I exist* is one of these, because it cannot be denied. You would have to exist to deny it, and your act of denying it would prove that you do exist. Logic alone does not dictate this conclusion, but your very existence provides evidence that cannot be contradicted by your words. These types of certainty admit no argument. There is no "getting behind" them to see if they are true; they are the truths behind all others and stand as self-evident. That is, they are evident in themselves and need no further evidence to justify them.

There are other types of certainty that are arguable. In each of these types of certainty, there are other possibilities, and the evidence must be considered. For instance, I have *virtual certainty* that I am sitting in my office. It looks like my office. These are my books, business cards, stationery, etc., and the file for this book was on the computer when I sat down. It is always possible, though, that I am quite mistaken. I might be hallucinating or imagining it all, or someone may have duplicated my office and be misleading me. However, since I have no evidence that any of these suppositions is true, it would be unreasonable to believe any of them. This is virtual certainty; it is possible that I am wrong, but there is no evidence to suggest it.

At last we come to *inductive certainty*, and this is what we really want to understand. Inductive certainty is possible when we have all the evidence and can draw a conclusion from it. This is called a perfect induction. For instance, I know that I have five fingers on my right hand. They have been there as long as I can remember, and their number hasn't changed. Furthermore, nothing has happened that would change the number of fingers I find there. Since I have considered all the evidence, this is a perfect induction and I can have inductive certainty. All the evidence is available, and it all agrees. But the only reason I can be certain of this induction is that I do have all the evidence. If it is not a perfect induction, there is no certainty, only probability. And probability, by its nature, is less than any kind of certainty.

Finally, there is *moral certainty*. This is an inner certainty that takes the form of conviction, but I may have to choose to trust some evidence over other evidence. For example, I can be morally certain that I am a new creature in Christ Jesus and no longer a slave to sinful desires. Now, some of the evidence I see suggests that I am wrong. I still look the same and, in many ways, still act the same, and I am sometimes influenced by dev-ilish impulses. However, the evidence of the Word of God tells me directly that I am a new creation (2 Cor. 5:17) and that I no longer have to obey those perverse desires (Rom. 6:8–14). Which evidence shall I believe? I choose to believe the latter because (1) it does not contradict the former, but tells me some-thing more about it, and (2) the Bible as the inerrant Word of God has higher authority than my own limited experience. In such matters, I have moral certainty.

Kinds of Probability

These are the kinds of certainty possible. But, as we have said, when dealing with induction, only perfect inductions can be certain. All other conclusions àre only probable, and we have listed the degrees of probability. But there are two kinds of prob-ability. The first is *a priori* or mathematical probability, and the second is *a posteriori* probability. They can be contrasted as fol-lows:

Figure 8.2

A Priori Probability	A Posteriori Probability
mathematical	empirical
independent of events	dependent on events
logical	scientific
statistical	experimental

A priori probability has to do with working out odds and possible combinations. It gives us a mathematical way to evalu-ate the likelihood of an event. A posteriori probability can be equated with what is popularly called the scientific method.[2] It gives us logical guidelines for working on inductive problems. It helps us ask our question, formulate a hypothesis, test that hypothesis through experimentation, and determine whether the hypothesis should be accepted or rejected. These are reasonable rules to help us find causal connections.

A Priori (Mathematical) Probability

There are various mathematical formulas for finding the odds of different kinds of events. For example, some events are simple and exclusive: either this happens or something else happens, like heads or tails when you flip a coin. Other events are more complex, like finding how many possible combinations of amino acids could combine to make the proteins necessary for life. Let's cover each formula by itself so that they will be easy to find later.

For exclusive events

If the event that you are studying is all by itself, not in combination with or dependent on other events, then it is called an exclusive event. For these the formula is really easy: just *count the number of possible outcomes*. A coin has two sides, so when you flip it, you have a 1/2 (that's 1-in-2 or 1-out-of-2) chance for getting heads. There are six faces on a die, so your odds for rolling a six (or a one, or a two, or a three, etc.) are 1/6. What are your odds of drawing the ace of spades from a deck of cards? If you said something higher than 1/52, you'd better count to make sure you're playing with a full deck. All other formulas just give us easier ways to count more complex problems.

For Independent Events

What if you want to roll two dice? Or flip two coins? These are separate and independent events. One has no effect on the other. In this case, we *figure the odds for each event to happen exclusively, then multiply them together*. If we are talking about coins, that means multiplying 1/2 x 1/2 = 1/4. There is a one-in four

---

2. It is not our purpose to convey that the inductivist notion of "scientific method" is the only method, but merely that it is a popular and well-known scientific method. In recent years this method has come under heavy criticism by philosophers of science. See *Christianity and the Nature of Science: A Philosophical Investigation*, by J. P. Moreland (Grand Rapids: Baker Book House, 1989), Chapter 2, "Scientific Methodology," for more information on this debate.

chance of getting two heads. Likewise, there is a 1-in-4 chance of getting two tails. But when it comes to the chances of getting 1 head and 1 tail, there is a 2/4 (or 1/2) chance, because two of the possible four outcomes have one head and one tail. If you are trying to roll two sixes with two dice, the odds are 1/6 x 1/6 = 1/36. What if you are flipping one coin and rolling one dice to get a head and a six? Then you multiply the odds for the coin (1/2) by the odds for the dice (1/6) and come up with a 1/12 chance. But does this still apply to drawing cards? No, because when you draw the first card, you reduce the odds of drawing a predetermined card on the second try, and so on (assuming you are drawing from the same deck and holding the cards already drawn from it). These events are not really independent, so the formula does not apply.

For Dependent Events

When we consider dependent events, we must ask how many different combinations are possible. We use the word *permutations* to refer to the number of possible combinations of things. The mathematical way to figure these is with factorials (you probably didn't expect a math lesson here). For a simple permutation, where we want to find how many combinations there are for a given number of known events, we multiply that number (n) by (n–1) x (n–2) x (n–3) and so on until we reach 1. Stated another way, we multiply every whole number between 1 and n together to find out how many combinations there are. For example, if we want to find out how many permutations there are for a string of three letters we multiply 3 x 2 x 1 = 6. If we get out some scratch paper, we can see exactly what these combinations are for the letters A, B, and T:

BAT	ATB	TAB
BTA	ABT	TBA

This can be expressed as three factorial (written 3!), but that doesn't really give an indication of what that number is. It is best to go ahead and do the multiplication.

If a magician passes out four cards to four people, there are 24 possible combinations of what order those cards might appear (4! = 4 x 3 x 2 x 1 = 24). If a security system has ten digits on the keypad and each is to be used once, then there are 10 x 9 x 8 x 7 x 6 x 5 x 4 x 3 x 2 x 1 = 3,628,800 possible entry codes. For you musicians, there are 479,001,600 possible twelve-tone rows (a series of notes that uses each step of the chromatic scale once). As long as we know how many factors are to be arranged, and each is only used once in each combination, this formula can give us the answer.

But what if that is not the case? What if we have several possibilities that might fit into each place in the series? This is called a complex permutation. Rather than a simple combination where each number is used only once, numbers may be repeated in a complex permutation. Instead of just punching in ten numbers in a specific order (a simple permutation), a complex permutation is more like the lock on a brief case that has three dials, each of which has the numbers one to ten. Any of those numbers can drop into any position in the series. So the total number of possible combinations is 10 x 10 x 10 = 1000.

Remember our BAT example? Well if any one of those letters can be used anywhere in the series, then our possible combinations expand greatly. Where we only had 9 combinations before, there are 27 now!

BBB	BBA	BBT	BAB	BAA	BAT	BTB	BTA	BTT
ABB	ABA	ABT	AAB	AAA	AAT	ATB	ATA	ATT
TBB	TBA	TBT	TAB	TAA	TAT	TTB	TTA	TTT

To figure the number of possible combinations for a complex permutation, you must *take the number of options for each position and raise it to the power of the number of positions.* Is that confusing enough for you? Put it this way: count how many different items could appear in each place in the series, then count how long the series is. Now multiply that first number by itself for as many times as the second number. Maybe we better try an example.

If you have a face-making kit that has (1) four possible noses, (2) four chins, (3) four mouths, (4) four sets of eyes, (5) four hair sets, and (6) four foreheads, then there are four options for each position and six positions in all. We take the number of options (4) and multiply it by itself the same number of times as the number of positions (6). So we get 4 x 4 x 4 x 4 x 4 x 4 or 4^6 (that's four to the sixth power), which equals 4,096. We can make 4,096 different faces. The easiest way to compute a complex permutation is just to remember OPTIONS^{positions}. Four options in six positions is four to the sixth power. A slot machine may have six characters that appear in each of three windows. So the possible combinations are 6^3 or 6 x 6 x 6= 216. Now, what possible use could all this be to any normal person? Does it have any relevance for what we normally think of as important? How about this: According to former atheist Fred Hoyle, in *Evolution From Space*, when the possible combinations are taken into account, the chances that the first living cell could emerge without a creator are about $1/10^{40,000}$. With odds like that, how can anyone deny that the universe was created and still be called reasonable? Likewise, astronomer Hugh Ross has figured the odds for the simplest life form to have occurred by pure chance. He says it would require a minimum of 239 protein molecules. Each of these molecules is composed of (on the average) 445 amino acids linked together. Now, each one of those links must be made by a particular one of twenty different amino acids. So the chance that even the simplest life form came together at random is 1 in $20^{445 \times 239} \div 239$ or $1/10^{137,915}$. Is it reasonable to believe that not only the simplest life form but all complex life forms arose from a fortunate accident?

Of course, many evolutionists know about these odds and say, "Well, given enough time, anything can happen." But is there enough time? Suppose the entire universe were made of amino acids (which is far from the truth). There would be 10^{77} molecules to work with. If we linked all these amino acids together at random at a rate of one per second for the widely accepted age of the universe (about 20 billion years), then the chances of that simple life form appearing shrink to $1/10^{14,999,999,905}$. That's roughly 1 in 10 to the fifteen billionth power! Twenty billion years just would not be long enough, even if the universe were packed with the building blocks to produce life.

To counter this attack, an evolutionist might respond, "But it only had to happen once! Being dealt a perfect bridge hand is a highly unlikely event too, but it has happened." This is true. It is possible; but is it probable? What is the degree of probability that the evolutionary hypothesis is true? David Hume said, "A wise man always proportions his belief to the evidence." All of the evidence says that the universe is too small and too young to permit the random assembly of life, even in a simple form. Following Hume's maxim, how can a wise man believe that life came about spontaneously and by chance when the evidence says that is virtually impossible?

On the other hand, what are the chances that Moses' record of creation just happened to put the events of creation in the right order? There are eight events (creation of the universe, light, water, atmosphere, seas and land, sea life, land animals, and man) which could have been put into any order. So this is a simple permutation and we figure 8!, right? ($8 \times 7 \times 6 \times 5 \times 4 \times 3 \times 2 \times 1 = 40{,}320$) Then the odds against Moses recording these events in the right order were $1/40{,}320$. Do you think he might have had some inside information?

If he did, then he is not the only one in the Bible who beat the odds. There are at least forty-eight prophecies in the Old Testament about Messiah. These include where he would be born (Mic. 5:2), how he would die (Isa. 53), when he would die (Dan. 9), that he would rise from the dead (Psa. 16), etc. The odds that 48 of these prophecies were fulfilled in one man are about $1/10^{157}$. That's right, a 1 with 157 zeros after it. Now, if a gambler had managed to guess forty-eight horses right without a single mistake, don't you think his bookie would suspect him of having inside information? The Old Testament prophets must have had some help to know so much about events that happened hundreds of years after their deaths. It is the only reasonable thing to believe.

All of these problems have answers where we can know the degree of probability by mathematical means. This is *a priori* probability. But we still need to discuss *a posteriori* probability, the kind where there are no numbers and you have to guess at how probable your conclusions are. Since this really involves a discussion of scientific method, we'd better just take it up in the next chapter.

Exercises for Chapter 8

8.1 Determine the average in the sense of mean, median, and mode for the following.

1. 1, 3, 7, 11, 23, 47, 52, 64, 70
2. 2, 4, 6, 6, 6, 10, 45, 78, 90
3. Books in philosophers' libraries:

Philosophers	Number of Books
2	2300
4	2000
3	1700
1	1600
1	1200
2	1000
1	600
2	500

4. Grades for logic students:

Students	Grades
2	100%
1	97%
3	95%
1	94%
5	90%
1	87%
8	86%
3	84%
2	80%
1	76%
2	73%
1	70%

5. Salary Structure

Employees	Salary
1	$100,000
2	$95,000
4	$85,000
3	$80,000
5	$75,000
2	$60,000
1	$50,000
7	$40,000
8	$35,000
6	$20,000
3	$18,000

8.2 Using the four basic questions discussed under the heading "Figuring Empirical Probability", determine if the following inductive arguments are strong or weak. If weak, explain why.

1. John, Bob, and I think the logic test was unfair.
2. We took a survey of the entire church and 90% of the membership is against a new building program at this time.
3. A brief look at several biblical verses will show you that I am right about this point.
4. We polled all the students at our Christian college and by the numbers we asked, it is safe to say that the majority of Americans are pro-life.
5. Several groups hold that the Holocaust never really happened, instead we're just being deceived.
6. Abundant historical evidence, both Christian and nonChristian, points to the fact that Jesus lived and died in the first century A.D. and that his followers reported his appearances shortly after his death.
7. I spent all day looking at the evidence and I still don't believe that God exists.
8. I spoke with every person of the eighteen except two, and none of them agrees with your version of the story.

8.3 Give the type of certainty for the following. Assume that all statements are true.

1. All girls are female.
2. I am a thinking being.
3. Abraham Lincoln was the sixteenth president of the United States.
4. Stealing is wrong.
5. I attend First Church in Dayton.
6. Jesus Christ rose from the dead.
7. People should be treated as ends and not as means to ends.
8. My eyes are blue and my hair is brown.
9. Triangles have three sides.
10. Logic applies to reality.

8.4 Using what we learned in this chapter, determine the probability of the following.

1. A book shelf has thirty books and you want a particular one. Selecting randomly, what is the probability of your getting the right one?
2. What is the probability in rolling four dice that they will all come up the same number?
3. What is the probability of drawing four kings in a row from a standard deck of fifty-two playing cards?
4. In a bowl that has three red ping-pong balls, four green ping-pong balls, and five yellow ping-pong balls, what is the probability of drawing a red ball on a single draw?
5. Returning to our bookshelf above, this time you want six particular books. Determine the probability of randomly selecting only those six books from the thirty books on the shelf.
6. If you flip a coin one hundred times, and fifty-five times it has come up heads and forty-five times tails, what are the chances that on the next time it will come up heads?
7. There are sixty-six books in the Bible, 1189 chapters, and 31,102 verses. What is the probability of randomly selecting a particular verse like John 3:16?
8. Returning to our bowl of ping-pong balls above; what are the chances of drawing two red ones in a row, not replacing the first ball selected.
9. Here is a telephone number: 555-4879. How many possible numbers are there in a single exchange (an exchange is the first three numbers)? How many possible exchanges can you have (remember exchanges do not use 0)? How many telephone numbers are possible without considering area codes? There are one hundred thirty area codes in the United States and Canada. How many possible phone numbers are there in these two countries?
10. One more trip to the bookshelf. Again you want six particular books, but this time you want them in a particular order. Determine the probability of getting all six in the right order

9

Scientific Thinking

In the last chapter, we began discussing inductive method. We said that you could know the probability of your conclusion either mathematically (if you already had all the data and they were limited to logical possibilities—*a priori*) or experimentally (if you needed to collect the data and the possibilities could not be predicted—*a posteriori*). The first method is stated as mathematical odds, but the second method is stated as hypotheses that are either confirmed or not confirmed by the evidence.

As Francis Bacon noted, science is the search for causes. The scientific search for causes can be divided into two broad categories: *historical* and *empirical*. The former deals with events that occurred in the past but are not occurring in the present. The latter deals with events of the present. The first category covers the origin of the world, and the second the operation of the world.

Scientific Approaches to Events Present

Scientific approaches to the present can be called *operation science* because they deal with how the physical and biological worlds operate in the present. These approaches have one thing in common: they can measure their views against a regular pattern of events that can be observed in nature. This is often referred to by the misleading title, "*the* scientific method." For many, "the scientific method" has become synonymous with knowledge itself. We have become convinced that whatever information is revealed by the hallowed name of science has a

"verily, verily" implied in its introduction. Science has given us
the substance of our lives—fuel-injected computerized automo-
biles, television, VCRs, compact disks, and microwave ovens.
But how many of us know what the scientific method really
is? Some may prefer simply to let the scientists do their magic as
long as we can reap the benefits. But if we are to be logical
thinkers, we should understand what they are doing to evaluate
their information for ourselves. It has often been said that you
can prove anything using the Bible. In the same way, the
authority of science can be abused by those who want to make a
fast buck, and the only way for us to know who is telling the
truth is to understand how an empirical scientist works.

Hypothesis-and-Testing Method

There are at least eight steps in this method. It begins with a
situation generating a question, then proceeds to state the problem, observe relevant data, reflect, formulate the hypothesis,
make predictions, test them, and evaluate the results.

Step one: The situation

The first step in the scientific method is to recognize a situation that is generating the problem or question. When the medical world realized how fast AIDS was spreading, it became very
important to begin looking for a cure. This situation brought
into focus a problem that had to be solved. Sometimes the problems are not so obvious. In some cases, a manufacturer just
wants to find some way to write "New and Improved!" on his
product. Also, some problems arise in theoretical sciences. There
may be no pressing existential need to know, but it can be helpful in general to refine the theory of relativity or to contemplate
the physical phenomenon of the Big Bang. Whether the problem is theoretical or practical, the first step is to recognize it.

Step two: Formulate the problem

The second step is to formulate the problem to be researched.
To say that you are going to find a cure for the common cold is
not enough. Where are you going to look? Will you study
germs, viruses, or the effects of cold weather? Exactly what
question do you want to answer? And how are you going to
look for that answer? What kind of study are you going to do:
statistical, experimental, historical, genealogical? Just as a student narrows down his subject for a thesis or a term paper, the

scientist must narrow his research to a bite-sized chunk that he can handle. He must decide which aspect(s) of the problem he has the ability and competence to study. This includes some idea of what kind of experiment he is going to do. If he doesn't know where he is going, there is a very good chance that he won't ever get there. The focused pattern of a shotgun can tear a hole through a barn door, but if you back up and try to shoot the whole farm, you are not likely to hit anything with enough shot to do much damage. If a scientist tries to study everything, he, too, is likely to have little impact.

Step three: Observation

Once the problem has been recognized and formulated, research can begin. All research starts with observation. Whatever relevant facts or data can be found should be noted so that they might provide some clue to the solution of the problem. This is where the scientist must be like Sherlock Holmes and observe every relevant detail. Reyes syndrome seemed to be a strange and deadly complication of the flu until doctors noticed that its victims had all been given aspirin to fight flu symptoms. It was the aspirin, not the flu itself, that caused the problems, but this never would have been known without some keen observation. You may not know what the significance of some piece of information is, but you must note it in case it becomes important later. Even the smallest clue may change the whole direction of your understanding.

Step four: Reflection

The fourth step is to reflect on previous knowledge. What has other research shown? What do we know about similar problems? What principles apply here that help us? These all become provisional assumptions—working ideas that we trust until they are disproven. We examine the things we observed in light of this knowledge and develop an hypothesis.

Step five: Formulate the hypothesis

Formulating the hypothesis is the central feature of the scientific method. The hypothesis is a statement of what we expect to find. It is usually defined as an intelligent guess about the way things work. Mind you, it is nothing more than a guess at this point. We have some observations and general knowledge to go on that have led us in this direction, but that doesn't mean we are experts yet. Our provisional assumptions may have been wrong, or we may have misinterpreted our observations. We might not even be in the right ballpark. A hypothesis is a way of stating what we think is going on, so that we can test to see if we are right. The type of thinking done in this step is neither inductive nor deductive, but adductive (like an insight). It is a speculation that leaps beyond what the available evidence can tell us.

Step six: Predictions

Testing the hypothesis gives us the next two steps. If our hypothesis is right, then what we are studying should behave in a certain way under certain conditions. (Notice that this is a deductive principle.) We should be able to make true predictions or deductions about the problem, if we have found some new truth. If our hypothesis is that fire cannot burn without oxygen, then taking away the oxygen should put out the fire. If the hypothesis is that snowstorms move in straight lines, then we should be able to predict where it is going to be snowing just by the movement of a storm. Remember, if the premises are true, then valid deductions must be true. So we need to see if our premise (the hypothesis) is true.

Step seven: Testing

The way we find out if the hypothesis is true is to test it by experimentation and further observation. We need to find a way to take the oxygen away from the fire (like a heavy blanket) or follow the path of some snowstorms. If our predictions come true, then we may be on the right track. If they don't, then our premise was false. There was quite a furor a while back about a pamphlet called *88 Reasons why the Rapture Will Come in '88.* The author had developed a theory of interpretation that certain numbers were very significant in prophecy (his hypothesis), and he made a bold prediction that Christ would come for his saints on a certain day in September 1988. His hypothesis was quietly disproved when the predicted time passed uneventfully. Experimentation puts our theory to the test to see if it works as expected. We will discuss later how experiments should be run.

Step eight: Accept or reject the hypothesis

Now that we have formulated the problem, done some research, and developed and tested a hypothesis, what comes next? The conclusion. The hypothesis has been either confirmed or disconfirmed. A good conclusion also states how consistent the results are, so that we know their degree of certainty. If the success of the hypothesis was in the 40 to 60% range, then further study needs to be done to see why there is such a discrepancy. If the results were less than 40%, it doesn't sound very likely that the hypothesis is right. If they were greater than 70%, the probability is good and the hypothesis is confirmed (at least to the extent of the probability). If the hypothesis is confirmed with a high degree of probability, then it can be accepted and used as working knowledge for new problems. That is, it moves from a mere *hypothesis* to a *theory*. (And if the theory is universally confirmed it becomes a *scientific law*.)

The Experimental Method

"How can we know what caused something to happen?" That is the question that the experimental method tries to answer. Experimentation is the method used to formulate and test a hypothesis. It is really five methods of testing for causal connections that help us determine what causes the effect and what does not. Some of these tests have both positive and negative sides. In each case, a negative test is more certain, because it tells us for sure that what we have tested *is not* the cause. However, it can't tell us what *is* the cause. For this, a positive test is needed, but the results of positive tests are only probable. It is always possible that another factor is entering the test and causing the effect, but we are not aware of it. We'll go over that again later and you will see how that works.

This method is not entirely foreign to us. If our television is not getting a good picture, we usually get up and play with the antenna. The problem is obvious, and our past experience tells us that the antenna can be out of adjustment, so we formulate our hypothesis quite quickly. We predict that if the antenna is moved in the right direction, the picture will get better. Next step: move the antenna. If our experiment works, we sit down and enjoy the program. If not, we can either formulate a new hypothesis or call the repair shop and let them do it. Any technical experts (repairmen, mechanics, doctors) will use the same experimental method to solve the problem, but they usually have more and better information with which to formulate their hypotheses.

There are a few terms that you need to know before we get started. When we talk about an *antecedent factor*, all we mean is *something that happens before the effect is seen.* It usually means, for us, the factor that we think might be the cause of the effect. It is the factor we are testing as a possible cause. The *effect,* of course, is *the event that we are trying to understand.* It is the phenomenon that brought up the problem in the first place and led us into the experimental method. A *concomitant factor* is *a factor that happens at the same time as the cause, but does not really cause the effect.* For instance, if, whenever I am thirsty, I bend my elbow to raise the coffee cup to my lips, I might conclude that bending my elbow relieves thirst. As it turns out, I can bend my elbow all day long without a cup in my hand and still be thirsty. In fact, if I have a twenty-pound dumbbell in my hand, I get more thirsty. This factor always happens at the same time as the real cause for relieving my thirst, but it is not the cause itself. Now that we have the terminology down, let's move ahead.

Method of Agreement

There are both positive and negative aspects of this method. Approaching this method negatively, it can be presented as follows: *no antecedent factor is the cause in whose absence the effect occurs.* In other words, the cause must be there to produce the effect. If the effect happens when the possible cause that you are testing is not there, then you are barking up the wrong tree. If you didn't drink a glass of milk before bedtime, then it was not the milk that made you sleepy. (But it does not follow that drinking a glass of milk cannot make you sleepy.)

Say your car is overheating. You take it to the mechanic and he says your water pump is shot, so he replaces it. The next day your car overheats again. The same effect occurred when the supposed cause (a bad water pump) was no longer present. You realize your mechanic was probably* wrong. (*But the water pump really might have been the cause the first time, and a new radiator leak the cause the second time.)

Job's friends had his problems all figured out for him. If he was suffering so much, then there must be some sin in his life. That was their simplistic theology: all suffering is caused by sin. They told Job over and over that all he needed to do was confess his sin and God would quit afflicting him. The only problem was that Job had not sinned. The alleged cause was not present in this case. There is no way that sin could be the cause for Job's suffering. His friends' whole idea of a God who causes suffering to punish sin came crashing down. Likewise, though death normally is caused by sin, Christ's death was not caused by his own sin, for he had never sinned. Therefore, his death was undeserved and can be credited toward others.

When the method of agreement is used positively, it says that *the single antecedent factor common to all situations where the effect occurs is probably* the cause*. (*There may be an unknown cause, and this common antecedent may only be a concomitant factor, not the real cause.) If you can show that there is only one possible cause that is present every time something happens, then you have a good chance of being right. For instance, when the common antecedent factor to lung cancer is regular use of nicotine, then nicotine is probably the cause. Psychologists and counselors started realizing that almost all of their cases with obsessive behavior or co-dependent relationships were people who had grown up in families where one parent was an alcoholic, or both were, or in otherwise dysfunctional families. Then they began investigating such families as a cause of compulsive behaviors.

In Alfred Hitchcock's movie *To Catch a Thief,* a string of jewel robberies followed parties in the victims' homes. There was only one man whose name appeared on the guest list of all the parties: the man played by Cary Grant. Since he had a record of stealing jewels, the police were certain he was their man. This is reasonable, and follows the method of agreement perfectly. Police today use this procedure all the time to narrow the field of suspects. However, in this case, there was another factor that was common to all the thefts. The same caterer had been hired, and the real thief worked for the catering service. The first suspect had only been there trying to prove his innocence. This is what we mean by concomitant factors that we are not aware of. You can't always be sure you have covered every possibility. It was thought for years that rats caused the bubonic plague that ravaged Europe in the Middle Ages. It turned out that fleas that lived on the rats were the real cause.

Method of Difference

This method reverses the method of agreement. Negatively, *no antecedent factor can be the cause in whose presence the effect fails to occur*. If it really is the cause, then it must be able to produce the same effect over and over under the same circumstances. If an unheated branding iron will not scorch a cow's hide, then it did not cause the brand mark on the cow. Either the cause or the circumstance must have been different. If a doctor gives a patient an experimental drug and the symptoms remain, then that drug must not be a cause of relief to those symptoms (i.e., it doesn't work).

The Church of Christ, Scientist, has practitioners all over the country who are legally protected to exercise their faith by treating illnesses without medical help. They believe that all sickness and death are only illusions. We simply have to affirm the truth of Christian Science that God is all, all is perfect, and we are truly perfect as immortal man, and we will be healed. If this claim were true—that is, if denying the reality of illness really caused healing—then there should not be any failure, given similar circumstances. However, the Christian Science maternity center in Los Angeles county was closed because of the number of women who had died there. An outbreak of measles at a small Christian Science college resulted in three deaths. One woman claimed that she had been healed many times of respiratory problems during childhood, but X-rays revealed that her lungs were a mass of scar tissue at age twenty-six. If the effect fails to occur in the presence of the supposed cause, then the supposed cause cannot be the true cause.

The positive side of the method of difference says, *in otherwise identical situations, the antecedent factor unique to one situation is probably the cause.* Again, there may be some other cause, but we have been through all that before. In this method, you keep isolating factors to see which one causes the effect. If you have allergies, the doctor can test by scratching you with a whole series of possible toxins, and whichever one you react to is the one to which you are allergic. One of the authors has a pancake recipe that always produces light, fluffy pancakes when he uses buttermilk, but they are flat and heavy when he uses whole milk. Do you think there might be a connection?

A man had a fifteen-year-old Peugeot diesel that was always surprising him. One morning, it would not start, so he began sorting through all the possible causes for this effect. He replaced a switch that he thought was bad. That didn't work. He replaced the battery. That didn't work. He replaced some bolts that were letting the engine push away from the transmission. Still no luck. He finally found out that his starter would work fine off the car using jumper cables, but would not work on the car. So he put it back on the car and tried to duplicate the conditions under which it would work, adding one factor at a time. He put the jumper cable to the positive post. Nothing. He used the jumper cable to replace the battery ground. Bingo! All the trouble turned out to be caused by a three-dollar battery cable that would carry enough power to run everything on the car except the starter. Once he isolated the possible causes and tested them one at a time, he could find out which one produced a different effect from all the rest.

Joint Method

The joint method is simply a combination of the first two methods. If you use both the method of agreement and the method of difference to test for a cause, then you are using the joint method and have a pretty good certainty that you really have found the real cause. This is a method of cross-checking. If you know that the television will turn on with the cord plugged in (positive method of difference) and that it will not turn on when not plugged in (negative method of agreement), then you can be pretty sure that you have located the problem. Likewise, when you have one antecedent factor that is common to all situations where the effect occurs (say, applying heat always makes water evaporate), and you also know that, in otherwise identical situations, the same factor uniquely produces that effect (stirring it doesn't work; dropping macaroni in doesn't work; putting it in the freezer doesn't work; but heat does), then you have two ways of proving that you have found the real cause. Ideally, all scientific evidence should be checked in this way, but that is not always possible.

Method of Concomitant Variation

Sometimes the answers are not just black and white. Some effects don't just either happen or not happen. Some things happen by degrees. Some light switches just turn the light on or off; others let you go from dim light to brightness and anything in between. You can be a little bit hot, a little bit angry, or a little bit hungry, but you can't be a little bit dead. When you are studying effects that vary, you have to study what makes them vary. The method of concomitant variation says that when one possible cause and the effect vary together, you may have found the cause. To state that in the same way as the other methods, *the antecedent factor that varies proportionately with the effect is proba-bly the cause.* Again, it is always possible that this factor and the effect are *only* concomitant—that is, that they simply happen together, but one does not cause the other. However, the rule generally stands that if your weight varies in proportion to the number of bags of Oreo's™ you eat, there is probably a causal connection.

We see this principle in people's spiritual lives all the time. Church attendance goes down whenever the weather is really bad and up when it is not. We all know Christians whose spiritual lives can be measured by the weather's evident effects on their behavior. One lady might gain weight when she is not spending time with the Lord, another might quit wearing make-up and let her appearance go. Someone might sing in the church choir only when he is having some spiritual growth. Others go the other way and become more obsessive about neatness and order as they let their quiet times slip into extinction. Wherever an antecedent factor varies with the effect, you have probably found the cause.

Now, this works not only with effects that vary but also in instances where there might be more than one cause for the same effect, or where the effect is viewed as happening within a large group of people. Some Scandinavian countries have a greater incidence of throat cancer than we do in America, and it was found to be related to the amount of peanut butter they ate. A mold that grows on peanuts in storage causes cancer, and it cannot be completely separated from the peanut butter. The more peanuts consumed, the more cancer appears. High blood cholesterol can be seen as one factor that causes heart attacks, but it is not the only cause, and the evidence that supports this conclusion comes from studies that show that societies where cholesterol levels are low have a low incidence of heart attack. The proportionality between antecedent and consequent factors indicates a probable causal connection between them.

Method of Residues

Another name for this method is the process of elimination. If you know what all the possible causes are, and you can eliminate all but one, then you have found your cause. More precisely, *the antecedent factor that remains after the other antecedent factors are found to be related to other effects is probably the cause.* An unknown factor may be the cause, so you can't say for sure. But when it is reasonable to assume that all the possibilities are accounted for, then you have a good case. If the only antecedent factor remaining, not attached to other effects (food, milk, air) is drinking water, then the public water supply is probably the cause of the public epidemic.

A historian named Frank Morison once took on the responsibility to discredit the gospel accounts of the resurrection of Christ on historical grounds. He found himself backed into a corner by the method of residues. The question for which he could not find an answer later became the title of his book, *Who Moved the Stone?* Was it the women? No, they did not know how they were going to move it when they came to the tomb Sunday morning. Was it the disciples? How did they get past the Roman guard? And why did ten of the remaining eleven die violent deaths for what they knew was a hoax? Was it the Jews? If they had the body, they could have produced it and disproved the claims that Christ had risen from the dead. Was it the Romans? The guards would be put to death for sleeping on their watch and would not want to implicate themselves. Besides, they also could have squelched the resurrection story if they had the body. Who is left, if not the angel from God, who the Bible said came down for that very purpose? All the other causes are related to other effects. The only option left is that God moved the stone.

These methods are the testing instruments of the scientific method. Without these, no hypothesis can be either confirmed or disconfirmed. They can give us both positive and negative knowledge of causal connections and can establish patterns to explain variations in the effect. While we can never say with absolute certainty that A caused B, we can at least give probable answers and test the connection in a variety of ways. This is the heart of a posteriori induction.

A Scientific Approach to Events Past

We have just looked at *empirical* science. It deals with the present. Its primary principles are repetition and *observation*. That is, a hypothesis can be tested by measuring it against a recurring pattern of events in nature. However, there is also a scientific approach to the past. It is sometimes called historical science. Archeology and paleontology fit into this category. So does much of astronomy. There is also a discipline known as *forensic* science. It deals with unobserved and unrepeated events of the past, like a homicide. Since the death was unobserved and cannot be repeated, the forensic scientists must reconstruct a *comprehensive* and *consistent* picture of it based on the principles of *causality* and *analogy*.

This approach to an unrepeated past event is called *origin science*, as opposed to *operation science*, which deals with a repeated pattern of events in the present. Since the past, unlike the present, cannot be known by direct observation, it must be inferred by way of the principles of *causality* and *uniformity*.[1]

The Principle of Causality

First, we must debunk a common misunderstanding of this principle. It does not claim that "Everything has a cause." The famous agnostic Bertrand Russell made this error in his book *Why I am not a Christian*. He argued as follows:

> If everything needs a cause, then so does God.
> If everything does not need a cause, then neither does the world.
> But in either case, we need not conclude there is a First Cause of the world.

The mistake is in the statement of the principle of causality.

Wrong statement: "*Everything* has a cause."
Correct statement: "Everything *that begins* has a cause."

Of course, if everything has a cause, then so does God. However, if only things that *begin* need a cause, and God has no beginning, then God needs no cause. Even Bertrand Russell, and many nontheists, believe the universe (cosmos) always was. As Carl Sagan put it, "The COSMOS is everything that was, everything that is and everything that will be." So, we can reply:

> If the universe does not need a cause, then neither does God.
> And if the universe needs a cause, then there is a God.
> But in either case, God is not eliminated.

1. See Norman L. Geisler, et al., *Origin Science* (Grand Rapids: Baker Book House, 1987) for further discussion on origin science.

The law of causality states simply that *every event has a cause.* Nothing can happen without being made to happen by something else. There may be events for which *we don't know* the cause, but we can be sure that *there was* a cause. *The Sound of Music* put it, "Nothing comes from nothing; nothing ever could." Any event that occurs must have a cause.

When the law of causality is applied to the *origin* of the universe, something interesting happens. It leads to a First Cause, which is generally called God. Consider the following:

Whatever has a beginning is caused.
The universe had a beginning.
Therefore, the universe is caused.

According to modern science, there is plenty of evidence pointing to a beginning of the universe. For example, the Second Law (not the hypothesis) of Thermodynamics declares that in a closed, isolated system (such as the physical universe), the amount of usable[2] energy is decreasing. But if the universe is running down, then it cannot be eternal. It must have had a beginning. So the first principle of *origin science,* the principle of causality, leads to a First Cause (Creator). By *Creator* we mean a powerful First Cause of the universe.

The Principle of Uniformity (Analogy)

But is this "Creator" intelligent or just a Blind Force? Applying the principle of uniformity to the origin of first life provides an answer to our question. For example, we know that coded messages (such as human language) are put together by intelligent beings. But if coded messages need an intelligent cause now, then we can reasonably conclude that they did in the past as well. This is reasoning by analogy, comparing the present with the past. It is called the *principle of uniformity* (or Analogy). The law of uniformity says that *the present is the key to understanding the past.* If we know how the universe operates now, then we can assume that it has always operated in the same way. If things that go up must come down, it is safe to believe that gravity was also in effect when Galileo was dropping things from the tower.

2. Only the *usable* energy is decreasing, since according to the First Law of Thermodynamics the amount of *actual* energy remains constant.

There are two possible kinds of causes for the origin of first life: a purely natural non-intelligent cause and an intelligent cause. The latter is called a primary cause and the former a secondary cause. For example, only secondary causes are needed to explain the Grand Canyon. Wind and erosion can easily be seen as the factors that cut the river's path deep through the rock. There is no need to suppose that there was any intelligent cause behind this. But what about Mount Rushmore? Did that happen by wind and erosion? Any reasonable person can see that a mountain with four human faces on it must have had an intelligent cause. It would be ludicrous to look for a natural cause for something that displays both complex organization and purposefulness. So for all singularities, we need to decide whether we are searching for a primary (intelligent) or secondary (natural) cause.

How do we know when to seek an intelligent cause? This decision is not arbitrary or capricious. In fact, it is based on the uniform experience of our daily lives. If you see "Drink Coke" written in smoke in the sky, you don't say, "My what an interesting cloud formation." You immediately know that it was put there by an intelligent cause. Why? First, you know it has a cause because of the law of causality. Every event has a cause, so this event must have a cause. But what kind of cause? Second, you know it has a primary cause because of the principle of uniformity. Whenever you have seen a design that carried complex information (or served a specific purpose), it was caused by intelligent action. After all, books are not produced by explosions in print shops; they have intelligent (or at least semi-intelligent) authors. TV commercials are not just a random assortment of lights and sounds that creep into your home by accident; they are carefully organized in every detail to make the product appealing to the audience. Now, a quartz crystal may have order to its construction, but it is not very complex. It just repeats itself over and over: FACE—FACE—FACE—FACE. And a string of random polymers has complexity, but it has no specific order to it: TICNBFG FJOS LXDIBN ROHNQ. Each of these occurs by natural causes. But only intelligent causes have both complexity and order, like this: "There is a message riding on this string of letters." It is our universal experience that wherever we see such a message, it had an intelligent cause.

The Principle of Comprehensiveness

A good hypothesis explains all the relevant data. For example, the old (nineteenth-century) creationist view that claimed all species were fixed and immutable is untenable. Small changes (micro-evolution) have been observed in nature. (Look at the difference between a Great Dane and a baby Chihuahua!) And changes have also been produced by crossbreeding. For instance, cattle and buffalo have been bred into beefalo (or cattalo). (They have not tried an owl and a goat to see if they get a hootenanny!) So any hypothesis that cannot account for all the known facts is inadequate. This is what led to the downfall of the creation-of-fixed-species view. A good hypothesis explains all the data.

The Principle of Consistency

Does our hypothesis contradict itself or other known facts? Any time there is a contradiction, there is an error somewhere. No two contradictory statements can both be true at the same time and in the same sense. For example, it is inconsistent to claim that everything in the universe is winding down but was never wound up, or that there is a cause for everything that begins but not for the beginning of the universe. It is also inconsistent to claim, as many evolutionists do, that life does not arise from nonlife, and yet that life arose from chemicals by spontaneous self organization. At least this is inconsistent if the present is the key to the past, as the principle of uniformity demands.

A Final Word

The differences in scientific studies of the *origin* and those of the *operation* of the world have been overlooked by most of the scientific community. This leads to confusion, since they deal with different objects and use different principles. A failure to distinguish these leads only to misunderstanding and misleading charges, such as, "Creationism is not scientific." Of course, creationism is not an *operation* science. But then again, neither is evolution, since neither creation nor total evolution deals with how the world *operates* in the present, but how it *originated* in the past. However, simply because neither creation nor macro-evolution is science in the *empirical* sense does not mean that neither is science in a *forensic* sense.

Exercises for Chapter 9

In each of the following cases, answer these questions:

  a. What is (are) the datum (data) to be explained?
  b. What hypothesis is proposed?
  c. What experimental method or methods were used in each case?

1. In September of 1846, two astronomers, J. C. Adams and U. J. J. Leverrier, discovered the planet Neptune. By studying the orbit of the planet Uranus, each man observed that the planet's orbit could not be accounted for by the gravitational pull of the sun and the planets orbiting within Uranus' own orbital path. Each man proposed the existence of another planet outside of the orbit of Uranus. Leverrier estimated the most probable position of this planet and began to search the heavens for evidence of its existence. Upon examining the star charts taken several nights in a row, it was noticed that one star changed its position from night to night. This star was the planet for which they had been searching.

2. By accident in 1879, Louis Pasteur discovered that the virus that had proven to be the cause of chicken cholera had decreased in virulence (the capacity of the virus to overcome bodily defenses) after having been left in a culture for a long period of time. Pasteur believed that there was a relationship between the time when new cultures of the virus were prepared and the length of time the cultures were allowed to stand isolated before they began to decrease in virulence. To demonstrate this relationship, Pasteur defined "the relative virulence of two strains as proportional to the relative numbers of deaths they produce in the same species when the creatures are infected in the same manner and under the same conditions."[3] It turned out that there was indeed a relation between time and the decrease of virulence.

3. One of the most often parroted objections to a capitalistic system is that it is the cause of imperialism. In this argument, imperialism is defined as the effort to extend the territory of one country by overtaking, through either violence or non-violence,

3. Rom Harré, *Great Scientific Experiments* (New York: Oxford University Press, 1983), p. 99.

the territory of another country. However, it can be demonstrated from history that many noncapitalistic countries were imperialistic in this same sense. Therefore, capitalism cannot be the cause of imperialism.

4. Nearly everyone has seen sleeping pets whimper, twitch their whiskers, and seemingly pump their legs in pursuit of dream rabbits. But are they really dreaming? Since animals can't wake up the next morning and describe their dreams, the question seemed unanswerable. But recently, Dr. Charles Vaughan of the University of Pittsburgh devised an ingenious experiment so animals could tell us, at last, that they were indeed dreaming. Rhesus monkeys were placed in booths in front of a screen and taught to press on a bar every time they saw an image on the screen. Then the monkeys were wired to an electroencephalograph machine and placed back in their special booths. Eventually they fell asleep. Soon the EEG was recording the special tracings produced by the dreaming brains of the monkeys. But most important, the sleeping monkeys were eagerly pressing the bars. Clearly they were seeing images on the screens of their minds—they were dreaming. Or so Dr. Vaughan believes.[4]

4. Irving M. Copi, *Introduction to Logic*, 3rd ed. (London: The Macmillan Company, 1968).

10

Fallacies in Scientific Thinking

Just as deductive logic has its fallacies, inductive logic has its set of common errors to be avoided. We said before that there are four different kinds of fallacies. There are formal fallacies, such as having more than three terms or an undistributed middle. There are fallacies of ambiguity, in which the meaning or relationship of the terms is unclear. There are also fallacies of relevance, which we often speak of as stacking the deck. All of these fallacies are found primarily in deductive logic (although they might occur in some deductive steps of an inductive study). The fourth kind of defect is fallacies of causal relations, and these are peculiar to inductive logic. They are the ways in which confusion can arise about what should be considered a cause and what should not. Induction opens itself to very specific types of abuse, and avoiding these fallacies can help to prevent that abuse from occurring. We will look at eight fallacies that can mar any inductive study.

Post Hoc Fallacy

The name comes from an old Latin phrase that sums up the problem: *post hoc, ergo propter hoc*—"After this; therefore, because of this." It *assumes that a common antecedent factor is the cause.* Because an inductive procedure always looks for the cause in an antecedent factor, it is easy to accept as the cause any antecedent factor that seems always to come along with the effect in question. The problem is that the mere fact that something happens before an event does not guarantee that it is the

166

cause. If it did, then every time the national anthem was played a ball game would start. The *post hoc* fallacy is like assuming that the sound of a rooster crowing causes the sun to rise. These factors are often present before the events, but it is clear that they are not the causes. Furthermore, the fact that every time we observe one event, we observe another before it, does not mean the other *always* precedes it. There may be some unobserved times when the antecedent is absent.

How might this fallacy happen? If one used the positive method of agreement without checking it with the negative method of difference, it could happen quite easily. This would lead one to find a given factor as a prime candidate for the cause of an event in question, especially if the real cause were not noticed in the experiment. However, the problem can be solved by testing to see if the alleged cause can happen without the effect following. Now, we have run several tests and managed to play the Star Spangled Banner without any sign of a football game, baseball game, or soccer match breaking out anywhere around us. We can also bend our elbows with forks in our hands without making our mouths fly open. Simply coming before does not mean that it is the cause.

In the Gospels, there are some strange things that precede Jesus' miracles, such as happened in the healing of a deaf mute in Mark 7:33–34: "And He took him aside from the multitude by himself, and put His fingers into his ears, and after spitting, He touched his tongue [with the saliva]; and looking up to heaven with a deep sigh, He said to him, 'Ephphatha!' that is, 'Be opened!'" Now, some have followed this as a procedure for healing deafness, as if these actions had caused the healing. But what really caused the healing? It is very likely that Jesus touched the man's tongue and ears just to communicate to him that these things were going to be healed. It is the power and authority of Jesus that healed the man, not touching and uttering, "Be opened." Just because he touched his ear *before* the healing does not indicate that this *caused* the healing.

Fallacy of Emphasizing Irrelevant Factors

This error is very much like the post hoc fallacy in that it is *confusing a concomitant factor (rather than an antecedent) with the cause.* It assumes that a *common* antecedent factor that happens to be present is the *relevant* factor when it is not. A cause has to have the ability to produce the effect. Flipping my hand upward does not generate enough power to make a light bulb run for several hours. What it does do, when it hits a light switch, is allow electricity to run the light bulb. The hand motion causes the switch to close, but it is not the relevant factor in making the light burn.

Like the post hoc fallacy, this error is likely to happen with the positive method of agreement, but it can also happen when noting concomitant variations. In both of these methods, we are observing a number of possible causes and trying to find the one that is always present with the effect. If we aren't careful to try all the possibilities and isolate factors as a test, then we might focus on the wrong concomitant.

For example, a drunk might start figuring, "Whether I drink scotch and soda, whiskey and soda, rum and soda, or bourbon and soda, I still get drunk." So he gives up soda!

In the first century, many thought that Jesus' physical presence was needed for him to heal their illnesses because they had seen so many come to him to be healed. So the woman with a hemorrhage sought to touch his robe (Mark 5:28), and the four men brought the paralytic to him (Mark 2:4), Jairus pleaded for him to touch his daughter (Mark 5:23), and sometimes all the sick in a city were brought to him (Mark 1:32). They seemed to believe that his bodily presence was the source of the power that healed. However, Jesus said that they were emphasizing an irrelevant factor. While he did not reject them for their misunderstanding, he said that his works were done by the power of the Holy Spirit (Matt. 12:28), and he gave his disciples the authority to do the same works (Mark 6:7, 13). Even more telling is the commendation he gave to a Roman soldier who said, ". . . just say the word and my servant will be healed." Of him Jesus said, "I say to you, not even in Israel have I found such great faith" (Luke 7:7, 9). This man realized that it was Jesus' authority, not his presence, that caused the healings. His physical presence was a concomitant, but not necessary and not the real cause.

Fallacy of Neglecting Negative Evidence

When a scientist loses objectivity and really wants to confirm his hypothesis, he might be blind to the evidence that tells him he is wrong. Perhaps he convinces himself that the exceptions are irrelevant, or just anomalies. Perhaps he simply fails to observe or make note of the instances where a common antecedent factor is not followed by the effect. But the problem can easily become an error in induction. Neglecting negative evidence means *overlooking instances where the supposed cause does not produce the effect.* This can happen easily when using the method of agreement, because you are not looking for differences then. It points out the need for using the joint method, because the negative method of difference could eliminate this fallacy: it tests this very thing.

An evangelist might preach that watching TV corrupts morals. He points to all kinds of instances where crimes seen on TV are reenacted in real life, or violent behavior is adapted, or the effects of violence seem unreal, etc. But he just might be overlooking many other instances where these effects are not found. After all, it is possible to use discernment in watching TV, and not everyone who watches will reenact the crime. If the evidence were taken as a whole, it might be very hard to support his hypothesis, for it is based on a minority of the evidence and neglects the negative evidence.

Fallacy of Neglecting Differences

It is possible *to confuse a similar antecedent factor with the cause.* This happens when one overlooks the fact that the common antecedent factors compared in different experiments are not identical. Oddly, this usually happens in the method of difference, because you are focusing on differences in the effect, rather than differences in the causes studied. Typically, this occurs when we assume that striking differences signal the real cause, but we should be looking for subtle differences. It is subtle differences between causes that will slip past us, not big differences in the effect. We have to be sure that the causes we examine are identical, not just similar.

Some overly zealous lovers of the *King James Version* of the Bible ("If it was good enough for Paul, it's good enough for me!") have noted that certain verses on the blood of Jesus are not found in the *New International Version* (e.g., Col. 1:14). They have concluded from this that the NIV is a "liberal" translation. They looked at the effect and saw a difference, then assumed that this difference was caused by the same thing that makes many liberal pastors play down or reject the doctrine of atonement. In this case, however, the cause was quite different. The fact is that the *King James* is based on a Greek text that was compiled from only a handful of manuscripts. Since that time, our knowledge of and access to older manuscripts has shown us that some words and phrases in the KJV were probably not in the original manuscripts of the Bible. Some verses on the blood happen to have been among those that were left out of the NIV, not to destroy doctrine, but to preserve the truth of the Scriptures as they were originally given. This is not a "liberal" trend, but a very conservative move to protect the Word of God from corruption. These causes might accidentally have the same effect, but they are hardly identical. Also, those who hold this view neglect the negative evidence that other verses on the blood are still included, even in the same chapters (see Col. 1:20).

Fallacy of Reversing Cause and Effect

This is a case of putting the cart before the horse. It *confuses the effect with the cause or the cause with the effect.* When the two happen almost together or as concomitant, it can be very hard to tell which caused which. This fallacy is even more typical when you can only assume which factor is really antecedent to the other. For example, at Podunk Bible College, it might be found that the students with the highest scholastic average are Christian education majors. The conclusion might be reached that Christian education develops the smartest people. But is that conclusion justified? It is just as likely that only smart people go into the Christian education department. How do you know whether the effect (higher grades) is caused by the department's program, or if the people were smart to begin with?

It is also possible that the graders in that department give higher grades or that the courses are easier. The conclusion fails to establish which is the causative factor. It doesn't even try to find which was antecedent, and that usually makes a difference. A cause must always exist *before* its effect. A father must exist before his son. The key must be turned before the car starts. The baking soda and vinegar must be mixed before they make a chemical reaction. Some studies, like the one at Podunk BC, don't indicate which came first. When we have that kind of data, where we have to view the events as if they were concomitant, it is very easy to make the error of confusing cause with effect.

Fallacy of Reciprocal Causality

Since we have already introduced the idea that identifying the cause may be difficult, there is another fallacy that is brought on by this confusion. Sometimes it is not a case of one thing simply causing another. Sometimes causality works both ways. The fallacy of reciprocal causality is *assuming that causality is only one-directional when it is two-way.* Usually, that assumption is valid. But not always, and particularly when you can't say which came first.

Take the relationship between violence on television and violent crime. Does watching violence cause people to do violent things? Or does television simply reflect the violence that exists in society? It may be that both are true. People with a tendency to violence may like to watch violence, which then makes them more prone to violence. As the brutality in society increases, so does the savagery on TV, and the two feed on each other. In this case, it is wrong to assume that causality can go only one way.

Why does an alcoholic drink? A recovering alcoholic and psychiatrist, John Bradshaw, says of himself, "I used to drink to solve the problems caused by drinking. The more I drank to relieve shame-based loneliness and hurt, the more I felt ashamed." The behavior was caused by the feelings, but it also caused the same feelings to intensify. Causality is not simple here. These events are interdependent and cause each other.

Fallacy of Confusing Cause and Condition

One error that we might fall into is not understanding what we really mean by a cause. There is a big difference between the things needed to set up an effect and making the effect happen. You can set the stage for a play, but until the actors arrive and the curtain goes up, the play doesn't happen. We speak of this distinction as the difference between a cause and a condition. A condition is a *necessary condition for the effect to occur.* It is the stage that must be set. The play cannot happen without it, but it does not cause the play. A cause is a *necessary and sufficient condition for the effect to occur.* It not only must be there, it is the one thing that makes the effect happen. Once the actors arrive, then both necessary conditions are met; when they begin acting, the sufficient condition is met also. Only acting is sufficient to cause the play to happen.

Let's say there is a grass fire in your front yard. After putting it out, the fireman comes to you and says, "It looks like what caused this fire was that pile of leaves you left by the road." Wait a minute! Since when can a pile of leaves start a fire all by itself? The dry leaves may have been a condition for the fire to start, but it was the cigarette thrown from a passing car that started the leaves on fire. The cigarette was the cause; the leaves were only a condition. A great deal of the false guilt that people lay on themselves for tragedies like this fire, or deaths in car accidents, results from people thinking that the conditions for the accident, over which they had control, were the cause of the accident, though they had no control over the real cause.

In a chemical reaction, there is a special kind of condition, which is easily mistaken for a cause, called a catalyst. The catalyst is a chemical that helps the reaction along, but it does not enter into the reaction itself. In some cases, the reaction may not be observable unless the catalyst is present. This may lead one to think that it is the addition of the catalyst that causes the effect, but it is really only a condition that makes the reaction possible. It is an environment that allows the effect, but it does not produce the effect.

The Bible clearly distinguishes a condition from a cause when it comes to sin. The first condition is the presence of a tempting object. Since we have such a propensity toward greed, envy, and idolatry, that could be just about anything. For our purposes, let's say it's a hundred-dollar bill sitting on the counter in a restaurant. Next comes the part that James calls being "carried away and enticed by . . . lust" (1:14). It is our sinful nature urging us to do what is wrong. Now, this is a part of our sinfulness, but we have not yet committed sin. This is a second condition for sin. Before we sin in relation to that hundred-dollar bill, we must start thinking about how much we could use it, that no one would see us, that it is really all right anyway, etc. In other words, we have to start desiring to sin before we sin, but desiring sin and deciding to sin are two different things. James says, "when lust has conceived, it gives birth to sin" (1:15). Being tempted is not sin; giving in to temptation is. Lust must conceive; that is, we must choose to follow our lust before we actually sin. Seeing the money and wanting the money are only conditions for our sin, but those things don't make us pick up the money. It is our own free will—our ability to choose—that causes sin. Temptation is only a necessary condition for sin. It is not sufficient to make us actually do the sin.

Fallacy of Confusing Various Kinds of Causes

When we have spoken of a cause in this chapter, we have used that word almost exclusively to mean the thing that actually does the job—the thing that produces the effect. However, this is only one kind of cause. There are really six different kinds of causes for any event. That sounds strange at first, but each of these causes refers to different aspects of the event.

For example, what is the cause of a chair? Actually, there are six different "causes" of the chair that we could consider. First, who produced the chair? This is called the *efficient* cause, and for the most part this is the way we have used the term in this chapter. It is the cause that makes things happen. In the case of a chair, that would be the carpenter who built it. Second, why did he build the chair? This is called the *final* cause, because it tells us to what end, or purpose, the chair was built (for sitting). Third, there is the *formal* cause, which answers the question, "What is the form, structure, or nature of the thing?" For our chair, we would have to call it `chairness'. It has a seat that is raised off the floor by legs, and a back to rest against (armrests are optional). That would be its formal cause. Fourth, what is the chair made of? This we call the *material* cause, because it tells us what kind of matter is involved. Our chair is made of wood, though other chairs might also be upholstered, plastic, or metal. Fifth, what pattern is followed when making the chair? This question asks for the *exemplar* cause, which tells us what the specific design of the chair is. Since our chair came in a do-it-yourself kit, then the blueprint that came with the kit is its exemplar cause. Finally, we come to the *instrumental* cause. What means were used to make the chair? This would be the saw, drills, and lathes that it takes to make the chair—the tools used by the carpenter. (Remember the grass fire we discussed before? What were its efficient and instrumental causes?)

The causes can be summarized by the following phrases with the example of the chair to help us see how they apply:

Figure 10.1

Cause	Description	Chair
efficient	that *by* which	carpenter
final	that *for* which	to sit in
formal	that *of* which	form of chairness
material	that *out of* which	wood
exemplar	that *after* which	blueprints
instrumental	that *through* which	tools

Now that you have an idea what we are talking about, let's discuss each cause individually to get a better handle on it.

Efficient Cause. This is what we normally think of when we say "cause." It produces the effect. Think of it as what gets the job done. For a fire, it is the one who started it. For the world, it is God. For sin, it is the moral agent. These are the ones who efficiently cause the thing to happen when otherwise it would not. Efficient causality may take two forms: primary and secondary. A primary cause is the first efficient cause of the effect; a secondary cause is a subsidiary efficient cause used by the primary cause to produce the effect. There is a primary cause for every event, but there may not be a secondary cause.

Suppose the boss wants a job done. He can either do it himself or tell someone else to do it. If he does it himself, then he is the primary cause and there is no secondary cause. If he tells someone else to do it, then he is still the primary cause, but he is acting through a secondary cause—his employee. God is the primary cause for all that exists, but he uses secondary causes (such as people, the laws of nature, and angels) to do many things in the world (like making chairs from trees, making new trees, and making axe-heads float when prophets lose them while cutting trees). For example, God gave the Ten Commandments to Moses, and they were written with the finger of God according to Exodus 31:18; however, the New Testament tells us that God used a secondary cause to do this, for it says that the law came through angels (Acts 7:53; Gal. 3:19; Heb. 2:2). The "finger" that God used was his angels. He used a secondary cause to accomplish what he wanted done.

Final Cause. This speaks of the purpose of an event or thing. It tells us *why* something happened, not *that by which* it happened. A chair is made to sit in. God made the world for his glory. A person is made to glorify God and to enjoy him forever. The final cause is the end for which the efficient cause acts.

Formal Cause. This tells us what form the effect takes. It tells us what the *nature* of the thing is—its essence; not *why* or *by which* it came to be. The nature of a human being is a physical/spiritual rational creature. The nature of the cosmos is limited, changing matter (energy). The nature of a chair is its particular form or shape. Hence, we call these the formal cause.

Material Cause. What is it made of? Not all effects have material substance, but most do have a material cause because they are made *of* something. A chair is made of wood. Persons are made of blood, flesh, and bones. The cosmos is the one exception to this, because it was created out of nothing (Gen. 1:1; Col. 1:16). Everything made since the creation has been made from something, that is, by re-forming material that already existed.

Exemplar Cause. Everything follows some kind of pattern. As Solomon says, "There is nothing new under the sun." It may only be an idea, or it might be a real thing that is being duplicated in detail. Everything follows an example, and this is called the exemplar cause. It is the *pattern after which* something is done. This does not refer to being after in time, but to being patterned according to. We need to be sure that we don't get this confused with the formal cause. A chair is made according to the design of its chairmaker. The cosmos was made according to a pattern in the mind of God. Ultimately, the pattern for creation is the ideas in the mind of God. Man, for example, was made in "God's image" (Gen. 1:27).

Instrumental Cause. The instruments used to produce the effect are the instrumental cause. These are the means *through which* the efficient cause acted. For the carpenter, it is the hammer and saw. For the cosmos, it is God's power and will. The instrumental cause God used in creating us was our parents.

It should be obvious by now that any confusion about what kind of cause we are talking about will change everything. Wood does not cause the chair in the efficient sense (unless "Wood" happens to be the carpenter's name). TV is not the efficient cause of crime, even when it is the exemplar cause. However, if you smash it on your kids' heads, it will be the instrumental cause of your crime of assault and battery.

Confusing Causes. Neo-orthodox theology says that the Bible is not the Word of God in itself, but that the Word of God comes to us through the Bible. They claim that the Holy Spirit may speak

to us in a special way while we are reading the Bible, but that
the revelation is directly from him and not in the words of the
Scriptures. This makes the Bible the tool that God uses to communicate with us. However, the Bible claims to be the Word of
God itself. In its words we are to find the revelation of God, not
in a mystical experience apart from the text. The neo-orthodox
confuse the instrumental cause with the formal cause. The Bible
is not merely God's instrument. The very nature of inspired
Scripture is that it is the Word of God. Revelation does not happen around or *through* the text, but *in* the text. The text is not
the means of revelation; it is revelation itself. God is its efficient
cause, using the human authors as a secondary cause. Its final
cause is the purpose (why) for which that message (what) was
written. Its material cause is paper and ink, and it is patterned
after the ideas in the mind of the author. Its instrumental cause
is the pen that wrote it and the words that were written (1 Cor.
2:13). To reduce what the Bible is to the status of an *instrument*
of revelation is a great theological error.

Some Bible expositors claim that the purpose for which the
Bible was written should be the guiding principle in our understanding of what the text means and how we should apply it.
But this method seriously confuses the final cause (purpose)
with the formal cause (meaning). For example, some say that it
is invalid to apply 1 Corinthians 5:5 to church discipline in cases
of wife swapping or adultery because Paul's purpose was to correct a case of incest. But does it really matter what Paul's specific
purpose was? Why not carry that a little farther and say that
Paul was addressing a specific situation and we can't apply the
passage at all? What Paul says (his meaning) was originally formulated in accordance with his purpose, but it does not follow
that we have to know his specific purpose to know his meaning,
or that we can apply his meaning only to situations identical to
the one he addressed. We don't need to know specific purpose
(why) in order to determine meaning. We discover meaning by
putting together all the little meanings of words, phrases, sentences, ideas, context, etc., to make a big meaning. We see how
all the little `whats' fit together to form the big `what'. When we
apply it, we don't demand that every circumstance of the first-
century context be repeated. We relate it by analogy to what is
happening today. Today's wife swapping and adultery is very
much like the case of immorality in Corinth, and Paul's meaning
can apply, even if his specific purpose does not.

One of the arguments often urged against the Christian God is that since God has determined all events, he must be responsible for all the evil in the world. After all, if he has ordained all things in advance and evil things have happened, then he must have ordained evil. The problem with this thinking is that it confuses primary and secondary causality. God is the primary cause of all things and, as sovereign, he is the primary cause of all events by knowing them from eternity and willing that they be so. However, many events are done through secondary causes. Among these are some evil events. God does not directly cause these things; he only allows them to happen without intervening. Being in control, he knows that they will happen and gives his consent to them, but the direct and immediate causes of them are the secondary causes that are employed.

At first, that may sound like a game of semantics, but this is a real and important distinction. Take the case of Job, where we know the dynamics of it. God allowed Satan to afflict Job twice, but each time with limits as to what could be done (1:12; 2:6). He *permitted* the affliction and set controls over it, but he did not *do* it himself. The evil was Satan's action and his own free choice. When God created beings with free will, he knew that there was a possibility for evil, but it was necessary to allow that in order to have creatures that were truly free. Even when God allows someone to do evil, she is still morally responsible for the evil that she does. A secondary cause acts on its own, not simply as a mechanism of the primary cause. Responsibility for evil must be given to the secondary cause that chooses to act in an evil way, not to the primary cause that allows the freedom of the creation.

These are the main causal fallacies. They are confusions about kinds of causes and causal relationships. Some are the result of not thinking through the problem well enough, and some come from not checking the results of tests. As long as these errors are avoided, induction is a good tool for finding probable conclusions.

Exercises for Chapter 10

For each of the paragraphs, discover which, if any, causal fallacy is operative.

1. My neighbor has had a disastrous year with his farm, yet I have had the best year ever. I have told him time and again to

read his horoscope every day. I think he is having these problems because he doesn't follow the stars. I didn't miss a single day of reading my horoscope this entire year, and look at how good my harvest is!

2. Ever since the Supreme Court decided to grant the accused more personal rights, the crime rate in this country has grown steadily. This clearly demonstrates that the increase of crime is the fault of the Supreme Court.

3. I never had problems with the air conditioner in my rental property until this most recent tenant. I'm sure he has caused these problems.

4. Shortly after the capture of the American ship *Pueblo* by the North Koreans, Richard Nixon made the following claim in a presidential campaign speech: "When a third-rate military power can capture a U.S. military ship on the high seas, it's time for a change in Washington."

5. Flying is a waste of time and money. I can't understand why anyone would want to fly rather than drive one's own car. There are frequent news reports about plane disasters, the airlines are constantly sending passengers' luggage to the wrong destination, and flights are never on time.

6. For the past several years the deficit of the federal government has grown. With the election of conservative Republicans, the deficit has not been reduced. In fact, it reached an all time high during the most recent administration. It is clear that the Republicans are causing the rising deficit by their policies.

7. In the Gospel of John, the apostle begins with a declaration of the identity of Jesus Christ as the Logos. In ancient Greek philosophy, the Logos was a prominent idea used to express the orderly nature of the cosmos. It is obvious that John developed his understanding of Jesus as the Logos of God from ancient Greek philosophy.

8. In our town, a local businessman has developed a program in the public schools to train young men and women to develop marketable business skills. Since the institution of this program, many of those who took this elective eventually became successful business executives. The plan is obviously developing the skills that are needed.

9. Pornography has increased in our country, and the lowering of the moral standard has followed. It is obvious that increased access to pornographic material has lowered the standard of morality in our country.

10. Down through the centuries men have killed and destroyed in the name of God. Indeed, it has been said that more injustice has been committed in the name of God than for any other reason. Atheism is a more human belief, because history demonstrates that a belief in God is the cause of much inhumanity to man.

Appendix
Truth Tables

Now that we have learned the different kinds of syllogisms and symbolic language, we can learn how to use valuable aids in determining if a proposition is true or not. We call these truth tables. A truth table tells us, given a proposition, whether others are true or false. You can symbolize simple propositions with letters. For instance, "All logic students are thinkers" becomes "S ⊃ T." However, in truth tables, simple propositions are symbolized by just one letter for the whole proposition. "All logic students are thinkers" becomes "S." Compound propositions are made up of two or more simple propositions. Therefore, two or more letter symbols are necessary (P · Q, P ∨ Q, P ⊃ Q, P ≡ Q). It is important that you don't get letter symbols for terms and letter symbols for propositions mixed up. In truth tables, letter symbols always stand for whole propositions.

Now let's examine these truth tables individually.

Negation

This first truth table is easy because it concerns a simple proposition. Let's take a statement:

1. "Jesus Christ is God."

There are two and only two possible truth values that statement can have—it is either true or false. Now if we negate the sentence:

2. "Jesus Christ is not God."

we still have only two possible truth values—true or false. However, notice that if 1 is true then 2 is false and if 1 is false then 2 is true. This can be placed in the form of a table:

Table 1

P	~P
T	F
F	T

Now *P* is what is called a statement variable and stands for any proposition. So if we substitute for it a symbol for proposition 1 above, say *J*, then our truth table looks like this:

Table 1A

J	~J
T	F
F	T

This is the standard table for negation and it never changes.

Conjunction

With conjunction and the other propositions, we begin to deal with compound propositions. The more simple propositions you put together in a compound one, the more possible truth values you have because each simple proposition has its own truth value. If a simple proposition has two truth values, then a compound proposition made up of two simple propositions will have four possible truth values. Since symbolic logic works in no more than pairs of propositions, our standard truth tables will never have more than four possible pairs of truth values. They are as follows:

Table 2

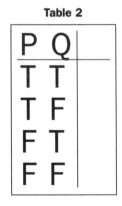

P	Q	
T	T	
T	F	
F	T	
F	F	

In conjunction, the standard table that never changes is:

Table 2A

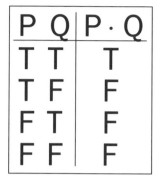

P	Q	P · Q
T	T	T
T	F	F
F	T	F
F	F	F

Notice that "P · Q" has only one truth value and we place it right under the conjunct symbol. This is how we will write all the compound truth tables.)

In other words, as we stated in chapter 4, the only time a conjunction is true is when *both* the propositions that make it up are true. If either of them is false or both are, then the entire proposition is false.

Disjunction

In disjunction we have the opposite of conjunction. For the disjunctive to be true, only one of the propositions has to be true (though both could be true). However, if they both are false, then the whole disjunction is false. The disjunctive truth table looks like this:

Table 3

P	Q	P ∨ Q
T	T	T
T	F	T
F	T	T
F	F	F

Hypothetical

Hypothetical propositions (sometimes called Implication or Material Conditional) are a little more complicated than conjunction or disjunction. The only time a hypothetical proposition is false is when the antecedent (the "If" clause) is true but the consequence (the "then" clause) is false. It would be helpful if we had an example:

If a person becomes a Christian, then he will be more moral.

It's obvious that if both the antecedent and the consequent are true, then the proposition as a whole is true. But what if they are both false? The hypothetical proposition would still be true, because the falsity of both the antecedent and consequent does not deny the truthfulness of the proposition as a whole. In other words, the fact that it might be false that a person becomes a Christian and the fact that it might be false that he will be more moral does not deny the proposition that *if* a person becomes a Christian, *then* he will be more moral. This proposition would still be true if nobody ever became a Christian or ever became more moral.

Nor can you say the statement is false if the antecedent is false and the consequent is true. It is possible for a person to become more moral and not become a Christian. However, if the antecedent is true and the consequent is false, then the hypothetical proposition as a whole is false. This is because the antecedent was not fulfilled by the consequent, which is what a hypothetical proposition is guaranteed to do. If a person became a Christian and didn't become more moral, then the proposition would be false. So, the truth table for a hypothetical syllogism looks like this:

Table 4

P	Q	P⊃Q
T	T	T
T	F	F
F	T	T
F	F	T

Biconditional

The Biconditional (also called Material Equivalence) is a symbol we have not encountered in any of the preceding chapters, so it needs some explanation. Look at the following propositions:

1. If you have paper, air, and a match, then you can have a fire.
2. You can have a fire only if you have oxygen.
3. You can have a fire if, and only if, you have fuel, oxygen, and heat.

The first proposition, a hypothetical one, states a *sufficient* condition for fire. This means that these three items are enough to have a fire. However, none of these items are *necessary* for a fire. I could have wood, coal, or dry leaves instead of paper; I don't need all the components of `air' like nitrogen or carbon dioxide; and I can use any source of heat like the sun, a blow torch, or a hot iron, instead of a match. We would symbolize this as we have symbolized our other hypothetical propositions: [(P · A) · M] ⊃ F. (By putting P, A, and M together in brackets we are joining them together in relation to F. Remember, in symbolic logic we always put propositions together in pairs; hence P and A becomes (P · A), and that joined with M becomes [(P · A) · M]. We can then join this whole group to F with our hypothetical symbol and get the pair [(P · A) · M] ⊃ F.)

In proposition 2 we have a *necessary* condition. You cannot have a fire unless you have oxygen. However, oxygen is not *sufficient* for a fire; otherwise, everywhere there was oxygen there would be fire. You need other things like something to burn and a source of heat. So while proposition 1 is sufficient but not necessary, proposition 2 is necessary but not sufficient.

But how do we symbolize "only if"? There are two ways. One way is to negate both the antecedent and the consequent and then to reverse the order: "If no oxygen, then no fire," or ~O ⊃ ~F. The other way (which is simpler) is to paraphrase the original proposition as such: "If you have a fire, then you have oxygen" or F ⊃ O. We simply make it into a hypothetical syllogism. Notice that we did not change the order of the propositions. Warning: a common mistake made by new students of logic is to ignore the "only if" and simply reverse the order of the propositions. It is incorrect to symbolize 2 as O ⊃ F.

Now let's look at 3, which is our *biconditional*. Here we have a *necessary and sufficient* proposition. Not only are fuel, oxygen, and heat enough to make a fire, but you have to have all three together in order to have one, and whenever you have them all together, you *will* have a fire. A fire is *equivalent* to these three components together. That is the meaning of the phrase "if (sufficient), and only if (necessary)." (Many people will use "if only" with the intended meaning of "if, and only if." Though this is technically incorrect, it is very common.) The symbol for a biconditional is three parallel lines: ≡.

What is the truth table for a biconditional? Well, P ≡ Q means that the simple propositions *P* and *Q* have the same truth value. So the only times when the proposition P ≡ Q is true are when *P* and *Q* are either both true or both false. If one is different from the other, then P ≡ Q is false. The truth table for a biconditional is:

Table 5

P	Q	P≡Q
T	T	T
T	F	F
F	T	F
F	F	T

Those are the only standard truth tables there are. Here they are all together:

Negation

P	~P
T	F
F	T

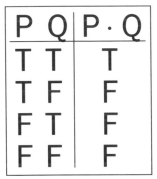

Conjunction

P	Q	P · Q
T	T	T
T	F	F
F	T	F
F	F	F

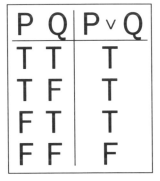

Disjunction

P	Q	P ∨ Q
T	T	T
T	F	T
F	T	T
F	F	F

Hypothetical

P	Q	P ⊃ Q
T	T	T
T	F	F
F	T	T
F	F	T

Biconditional

P	Q	P ≡ Q
T	T	T
T	F	F
F	T	F
F	F	T

Glossary

A Posteriori. From experience; dependent on experience, as opposed to *a priori* (see).

A Posteriori Probability. Probability that is confirmed by appeal to evidence and experimentation.

A Priori. Prior to or independent of experience, as opposed to *a posteriori* (see).

A Priori Probability. Probability that is known in advance of experience, purely mathematical or logical.

Ab Annis. Fallacy of appealing to age as determinative of the truth of a statement.

Ad Baculum. Fallacy of appealing to force or fear of harm as determinative of the truth of an argument.

Ad Futuris. Fallacy of appealing to some possible future state of affairs as determinative of the truth of a claim.

Ad Hominem. Fallacy of appealing in some manner to an individual as determinative of the truth of an argument instead of relevant information. There are two forms: *abusive*, which is an attack on the person's character, and *circumstantial*, which is an attack on the person's circumstances.

Ad Ignorantiam. Fallacy of appealing to a person's ignorance of an issue as determinative of the truth of his statement.

Ad Misericordiam. Fallacy of appealing to pity as determinative of the truth of an argument.

Ad Populum. Fallacy of appealing to popular and fashionable ideas as determinative of a truth claim.

Ad Verecundiam. Fallacy of appealing to an inappropriate authority as determinative of the truth of an argument.

Amphibole. Fallacy of unclear grammatical construction that creates difficulty in determining the meaning and truth of a statement.

Antecedent. The conditional element in a hypothetical statement as in, "If A, then B" (see *Consequent*).

Antecedent Factor. A preceding event, condition, or cause that may or may not have determined a specific effect.

Argument. The presentation of reasons for inferring a particular conclusion.

Argument of the Beard. Fallacy of presuming that there is no real difference between the extremes on a continuum because the differences between adjacent positions along the continuum are almost imperceptible.

Begging the Question. Fallacy of reasserting the conclusion of an argument in the premises, called *Petitio Principii* (see).

Categorical Proposition. A proposition that affirms or denies something, taking the form of a declarative sentence.

Categorical Syllogism. A syllogism made up of three categorical propositions, two of which are premises and one is a conclusion.

Category Mistake. Fallacy of confusing things from one category of ideas or items to an unrelated category of ideas or items.

Cause. A necessary and sufficient condition for an effect to occur. (But see Chapter 10 for a discussion of various types of causes.)

Cliche. A generalized and overused phrase; when used in logic it is the fallacy of appealing to a cliche as determinative of truth.

Complex Question. Fallacy that occurs when a question that really contains two or more questions is asked, and a single answer is expected.

Compound Syllogism. A syllogism that is composed of different types of propositions other than just categorical propositions.

Concomitant Factor. An event that occurs at the same time as, but is not the cause of, a specific effect.

Conjunctive Syllogism. A syllogism that is composed of a conjunctive statement as the single premise ("both/and") and that yields two conclusions by separating the two conjuncts.

Consensus Gentium. Fallacy of appealing to majority opinion as determinative of the truth of that issue.

Consequent. The conclusion of a hypothetical statement, as in "If A, then B," (see *Antecedent*).

Constructive Dilemma. A dilemma form of an argument where the two consequents are affirmed in the conclusion, as in: If P then Q and if R then S, P or R, therefore Q or S (see *Destructive Dilemma*).

Contradiction. One or more propositions that assert or (imply) both the truth and falsity of something.

Contraposition. A logical operation that creates an equivalent proposition by first obverting a categorical proposition, then converting the obversion, and finally obverting the conversion (see *Obversion* and *Conversion*).

Contrariety. Occurs when the truth of one proposition involves the falsity of the other but the falsity of one of the propositions does not necessarily involve the truth of the other; where two propositions cannot both be true, but they could both be false (see *Square of Opposition*).

Conversion. A logical process by which an equivalent proposition is created by switching the subject and predicate terms in a categorical proposition. Type A propositions convert to Type I, Type E to Type E, and Type I to Type I. Type O propositions do not convert.

Copula. Any form of the verb "to be" in a standard categorical proposition.

Deductive Argument. An argument where (if valid) the conclusion follows necessarily from the premises; arguing from a general concept to a particular situation.

Destructive Dilemma. A dilemma form of an argument where the two antecedents are denied in the conclusion, as in: If P then Q and if R then S, ~(Q ∨ S), therefore ~(P ∨ R) (see *Constructive Dilemma*).

Dicto Simpliciter. Fallacy of applying a general rule to a specific case when significant differences exist that render the rule inapplicable.

Dilemma Form. An argument presenting two possible options where you must choose one over the other; placed in the form of two hypothetical statements in conjunction together where either the antecedents are denied in the conclusion or the consequents are affirmed in the conclusion, respectively (see *Constructive Dilemma* and *Destructive Dilemma*).

Disjunctive Proposition. A proposition made up of two terms, called alternants, that are in opposition to each other; placed in the form of "either/or."

Disjunctive Syllogism. A syllogism made up of a disjunctive statement in the first premise, a denial of either one or the other alternants in the second premise, and the affirmation of the other alternant in the conclusion.

Distribution. An attribute possessed by a term in a categorical proposition describing its relationship to the entire class denoted by the term. Distribution may be particular (denoting only some of the class) or universal (denoting all of the class).

Efficient Cause. The cause that produces an effect; that *by which* an effect is produced, as opposed to *final* or *instrumental* causes (see).

Empirical Probability. The examination of empirical evidence to determine the probable conclusion in an inductive situation.

Enthymeme. A categorical syllogism that is missing either a premise or the conclusion.

Equivalence. Two statements that have identical meanings.

Equivocation. A fallacy that occurs when a term changes its meaning within an argument.

Exceptive Proposition. A categorical proposition that states exceptions using terms like "All except" and "All but."

Exclusive Premises. A formal fallacy that occurs when both premises of a categorical syllogism are negative.

Exclusive Proposition. A categorical proposition that makes an exclusive claim using terms like "Only" and "None but."

Exemplar Cause. The pattern *after which* something is done.

Experimental Method. The method used to formulate and test a hypothesis through experimentation.

Fallacies of Ambiguity. The collection of informal fallacies that are guilty of unclear communication.

Fallacies of Relevance. The collection of informal fallacies that are guilty of introducing irrelevant information into an argument.

Fallacy of Accent. Fallacy that occurs due to a lack of clarity in the emphasis or tone of voice of a proposition.

Fallacy of Composition. Fallacy that assumes that what is true of the parts is true of the whole.

Fallacy of Division. Fallacy that assumes that what is true of the whole is true of the parts.

Faulty Analogy. Fallacy that employs an analogy that is irrelevant to the argument in any significant sense.

Faulty Dilemma. Fallacy that occurs when two options are presented as exclusive while other alternatives are available.

Figure. A designation of where the middle term appears in a categorical syllogism.

Final Cause. The purpose of an effect; that *for which* something happened, as opposed to *efficient* or *instrumental* cause (see).

Formal Cause. The form an effect takes; that *of which*, as opposed to *material cause* (see).

Formal Fallacy. A fallacy that occurs due to the form or structure of an argument.

Formal Logic. The division of logic that deals with the form and structure of logical arguments.

Four-Term Fallacy. A formal fallacy that occurs when there are four terms in a categorical syllogism instead of three.

Genetic Fallacy. Fallacy that appeals to the source of a view or belief as determinative of its truthfulness.

Hasty Generalization. Fallacy that occurs when a general conclusion is drawn from either atypical or not enough specific cases.

Hypothesis. Conjecture offered as a possible solution to a problem.

Hypothesis Contrary to Fact. Fallacy of appealing to what could possibly have been the case, rather than what was the case.

Hypothetical Proposition. A conditional statement claiming that if one state of affairs is true, then another state of affairs will follow.

Hypothetical Syllogism. A syllogism made up of a hypothetical proposition in the first premise, either the antecedent is affirmed or the consequent is denied in the second premise, and the other is affirmed or denied, respectively, in the conclusion.

Ignoratio Elenchi. Fallacy of appealing to an irrelevant premise or conclusion as determinative of the truth of an argument.

Illicit Process. A formal fallacy that occurs when a term is distributed (universal) in the conclusion but not in the premises; when it is the major term it is called *Illicit Major* and when it is the minor term it is called *Illicit Minor*.

Immediate Deduction. A deduction that can be drawn directly from a statement without knowing anything else.

Independence. Relationship between propositions when the truth or falsity of one has no bearing on the truth or falsity of the other.

Inductive Argument. An argument where the conclusion follows with some degree of probability from the premises; moves from particular to general, as opposed to *deductive* (see).

Inductive Certainty. Certainty that is possible when we have all the evidence and can draw a conclusion.

Informal Fallacy. A fallacy that occurs due to the content of an argument.

Instrumental Cause. The means *through which* an efficient cause acts, as opposed to an *efficient cause* (see).

Joint Method. Occurs when one uses both the *Method of Agreement* and the *Method of Difference* in testing a hypothesis by the *experimental method* (see).

Law of Excluded Middle. Law of logic that excludes any middle alternative between alternatives; either A or non-A.

Law of Identity. Law of logic that states that something is itself; A is A.

Law of Non-Contradiction. Law of logic that states that something cannot both be and not be at the same time and in the same respect; A is not non-A.

Laws of Rational Inference. Laws of logic that allow inferences to be reached from a series of premises to a conclusion.

Logic. The study of right reason or valid inferences and the attending fallacies, formal and informal.

Logical Certainty. The kind of certainty that is possible based on the law of non-contradiction.

Major Term. The term that is in the predicate of the conclusion in a standard categorical syllogism and appears in (defines) the major premise.

Material Cause. The substance from which something is made; that *out of* which it is composed, as opposed to *formal cause* (see).

Material Logic. The division of logic that deals with the truthfulness of the content of an argument.

Mathematical Certainty. Something that is certain because it is true by definition or its only alternative is contradictory.

Mean. The statistical average of a group of numbers.

Median. The halfway number in a group of numbers.

Mediate Deduction. A deduction that can be drawn from one proposition to another through the way of a third proposition (i.e., a *syllogism*).

Method of Agreement. In using the *experimental method* (see), no antecedent factor can be the cause in whose absence the effect occurs.

Method of Concomitant Variation. In using the *experimental method* (see), the antecedent factor that varies proportionately with the effect is probably the cause.

Method of Difference. In using the *experimental method* (see), no antecedent factor can be the cause in whose presence the effect fails to occur.

Method of Residues. In using the *experimental method* (see), the antecedent factor that remains after the other antecedent factors are found to be related to other effects is probably the cause; the process of elimination.

Middle Term. The term that is located in both the premises but not in the conclusion of a categorical syllogism.

Minor Term. The term that is the subject of the conclusion in a categorical syllogism and also appears once in the minor premise.

Mode. The number that occurs most frequently in a group of numbers.

Modus Ponens. A rule of inference used in a hypothetical syllogism where the antecedent is affirmed in the premise leading to the affirmation of the consequent in the conclusion, as in: If P then Q, P, therefore Q.

Modus Tollens. A rule of inference used in a hypothetical syllogism where the consequent is denied in the premise leading to the denial of the antecedent in the conclusion, as in: If P then Q, not-Q, therefore not-P.

Mood. A designation in a categorical syllogism of the order of the types of propositions (A, E, I, O) that make it up.

Moral Certainty. An inner certainty, less than *mathematical certainty,* that takes the form of a moral conviction.

Necessary Condition. A condition that must obtain in order for an effect to occur (see *Sufficient Condition*).

Non Sequitur. A fallacy where the conclusion does not follow from the premises.

Obversion. A logical operation that creates an equivalent proposition by changing the quality and negating the predicate of a categorical proposition. Propositions of Type A obvert to Type E; Type E to Type A; Type I to Type O; and Type O to Type I.

Operation Science. Term describing how science approaches the ongoing functioning of the physical universe using the *experimental method* (see).

Origin Science. Term describing how science approaches studies of the past (e.g., origin of the physical universe or living things) using the principles of uniformity and causality (see).

Particular Statement. A statement that makes a claim about one or more, but not all, members of a class.

Petitio Principii. Fallacy of reasserting the conclusion of an argument in the premises, sometimes called *Begging the Question* (see).

Post Hoc Fallacy. Fallacy that confuses a universally observed antecedent factor with the cause; sometimes called false cause.

Predicate Term. The term that follows the copula ("is" or "is not") in a categorical proposition to which the subject is related.

Premise. A proposition in an argument that sets forth a reason or evidence for the conclusion.

Prescriptive. A non-argumentative statement or series of statements commanding or prescribing something.

Prestige Jargon Fallacy. Fallacy of appealing to complicated or technical language as determinative of the truth of an argument.

Principle of Causality. The principle that every event has a cause.

Principle of Comprehensiveness. The principle that the best hypothesis is that which best explains all the data.

Principle of Consistency. The principle that a hypothesis is ruled out if it contradicts itself or is inconsistent.

Principle of Uniformity. The principle that the present is key to the past, that the way things occur in the present is the key to understanding their occurrence in the past.

Probability. Something that is supported by evidence strong enough to establish presumption, but not necessarily a proof.

Proposition. In logic, a declarative statement that affirms or denies something, having a *subject term, copula,* and *predicate term* (see).

Quantifier. The term that refers to the extent of the class of the subject term in a categorical syllogism, whether *universal* or *particular* (see).

Reciprocal Causality. Fallacy in scientific thinking that assumes that causality is one directional when it is in fact two-way.

Red Herring. Fallacy that occurs by diverting attention to an extraneous issue rather than providing evidence for the claim.

Slippery Slope Fallacy. Fallacy that occurs when it is assumed that accepting the conclusion of an argument will set off a chain of undesirable consequences, when in fact there is no reason to believe that this reaction will occur.

Sorite. A series of categorical syllogisms in which the intermediate conclusions have been left out; an extended syllogism.

Sound Argument. A deductive argument that is both *valid* (see) and *true.*

Special Pleading. Fallacy of applying a double standard that emphasizes one's own position as correct and others as incorrect.

Square of Opposition. A diagram that exhibits the necessary relations that prevail between the four types (A, E, I, O) of categorical propositions. (See *Contradiction, Contrariety, Subalternation, Subcontrariety, Superalternation*)

Statistical Probability. The use of mathematical formulas to calculate probability.

Straw Man. Fallacy of establishing a position, claiming it is the opponent's position, and then attacking it, when it is not in fact the opponent's position at all.

Subalternation. Occurs when the truth of one categorical proposition does not necessarily involve the truth of another, but the falsity of one does involve the falsity of the other. (See *Square of Opposition*)

Subcontrariety. Occurs when the truth of one categorical proposition does not necessarily involve the falsity of the other but the falsity of one does involve the truth of the other. (See *Square of Opposition*)

Subject Term. The term that precedes the *copula* (see) in a categorical proposition and establishes what the proposition is about.

Sufficient Condition. A condition that is adequate for an effect to occur, as opposed to a *necessary condition* (see).

Superalternation. Occurs when the truth of one categorical proposition involves the truth of another, but the falsity of one does not necessarily involve the falsity of the other. (See *Square of Opposition*)

Syllogism. A deductive argument consisting of premises and a conclusion.

Tautology. A statement that is necessarily true by either definition or logical form.

Undeniability. That which cannot be actually (existentially) or logically denied without implied self-contradiction.

Undistributed Middle. A formal fallacy that occurs when the middle term of a categorical syllogism is not distributed at least once in the premises.

Universal Statement. A statement that makes an assertion about all the members of the class to which the subject term refers.

Validity. A characteristic of the form of an argument, not its content; a deductive argument where it is impossible for the premises to be true and the conclusion to be false; an argument in which none of the laws of inference are broken.

Virtual Certainty. Almost entire certainty of something, but not complete certainty as in logical or mathematical certainty.

Bibliography

Copi, Irving I. *Introduction to Logic.* Sixth ed. New York: Macmillan, 1982.

Engel, S. Morris. *With Good Reason: An Introduction to Informal Fallacies.* Third ed. New York: St. Martins, 1986.

Hoover, A. J. *Don't You Believe It!* Chicago: Moody, 1982.

Hurley, Patrick J. *Logic.* Third ed. Belmont, Calif.: Wadsworth, 1988.

Ruby, Lionel. *Logic: An Introduction.* Chicago: J. B. Lippincott, 1960.

Answer Key to Exercises

Chapter 2

2.1 Is it an argument?
1. Inductive
2. No argument
3. Deductive
4. No argument
5. Deductive
6. Inductive
7. No argument
8. Deductive
9. No argument
10. Inductive

2.2 Identify four terms in categorical proposition.

    Q   S   C   P
1. [All] [Christians] [are] [saved].

    Q   S   C   P
2. [No] [Baptists] [are] [Presbyterians].

      Q   S   C   P
3. [Some] [people who attend church] [are not] [true believers].

        S   C   P
4. [Salvation] [is] [a free gift]. (Q implied)

        S   C   P
5. [Bertrand Russell] [is] [an atheist]. (Q implied)

    Q   S   C   P
6. [Some] [atheists] [are] [communists].

        S   P
7. [David Hume] [wrote an argument against believing in miracles]. (Q & C implied)

    Q   S   C   P
8. [All] [communists] [are] [atheists].

    S
9. [Christians who study their Bibles, pray, and obey
    Christ],   P
    [will remain in fellowship with God].   (Q & C implied)
    Q   S   P
10. [No] [nonbelievers] [will go to heaven].   (C implied)
        S   P
11. [God] [does not change].   (Q & C implied)
    S   C   P
12. [I] [am not] [an atheist].   (Q implied)
    Q   S   C   P
13. [All] [people] [are] [descendants of Adam].
        Q   S   C   P
14. [Some] [descendants of Adam] [are] [believers in
    Christ].
        Q   S   C   P
15. [Some] [people] [are not] [believers in Christ].

2.3 Universal/Particular & Affirmative/Negative
1. PA
2. UN
3. PN
4. UA
5. UA
6. UN
7. This is the first time we have a proposition that has no
   copula, so we must supply one. Change the sentence to
   "Some angels *are beings who fell with Satan.*" Now it
   becomes a PA proposition.
8. Translate to "God is one who cannot sin." :UA
9. UA
10. Propositions that begin with "None" by itself are treated
    as if they began with "No one" and are negative. This
    proposition is UN. However, if a proposition begins with
    "None but," then it is an exclusive proposition like
    "Only." See exercise 2.6, #8 for handling exclusive
    propositions.
11. PN
12. PA
13. UN
14. This can be either UN or PN depending on how one sees
    it. Because "All . . . are not . . ." really means "Not

all are . . . ," or "Some . . . are not . . . ," we will
always interpret these as PN. It might help if you rewrite
the sentence each time you see it.

15. UA
16. PA. Terms like *many* and *most* are just greater *somes*.

2.4 A, E, I, and O propositions

1. E
2. A
3. O
4. A
5. I
6. A
7. E
8. A
9. E. "They" = "[all] the people in this group to which I refer."
10. A. See #9.
11. O. See 2.3, #14.

2.5 A, E, I, and O propositions & distribution

1. A: Distributed (D), Undistributed (U)
2. E: D, D
3. Simple identity; Note the exclusive definite article.
4. A: D, U
5. I: U, U
6. I: U, U
7. I: U, U; "Most" is not all, but is only some.
8. O: U, D; Remember "All . . . are not . . ." rule (2.3, #14)
9. E: D, D
10. O: U, D
11. A: D, U
12. A: D, U
13. O: U, D
14. E: D, D
15. Because this is missing the copula, it can be difficult to
figure out. It can actually be stated two different ways.
The easiest is "Immoral persons *are persons who* can't be
trusted." It would then be A: D, U. However you can
also say "Immoral persons *are not persons you can trust*"
which would be E: D, D. Although either would be

acceptable, in general, you should use the one that changes the original the least.

2.6 For advanced students

1. A: D, U; just insert a copula.
2. A: D, U
3. E: D, D; "Some person" is singular (not "Some persons") and for our purposes, singulars are always treated as universals.
4. O: U, D
5. A: D, U; the `not' here modifies the subject term, not the copula.
6. A: D, U; same as above
7. A: D, U; "something" is singular.
8. This is what is called an exclusive sentence. Another way to put it would be "Only believers will go to heaven." Exclusive sentences need to be changed into an A, E, I, or O proposition before we can work with them. This is a two-step process: 1) change "only" or "none but" to "all" and 2) switch the subject and the predicate terms. So our original sentence becomes "All who go to heaven are believers," which is A: D, U.
9. This is what is called an exceptive sentence. It also needs to be changed into an A, E, I, or O proposition. However, we have a couple of different options to choose from. This example could be translated, "All who are not George became Christians at last night's meeting," which would be A: D, U (the "are not" here is modifying the subject term, not the copula). It could be translated, "George is not someone who became a Christian at last night's meeting," which is E: D, D. There is no preference for which you use, either will work.
10. Same as #8; "All the answers to the world's problems are answers found in Jesus"; A: D, U

Chapter 3

3.1 Identifying terms and premises
m   mid
1. All agnostics deny any knowledge of God.   (m)

　　　　　mid   M
Those who deny any knowledge of God do not make
sense. (M)
　　　m   M
Agnostics do not make sense.

　　　　m   mid
2. Some people attend church. (m)
　　　　M   mid
　　All Christians attend church. (M)
　　　　m   M
　　Some people are Christians.

　　　　　mid   M
3. Everything that has a beginning must have had a
cause. (M)
　　　　　m   mid
　　The universe had a beginning. (m)
　　　　　m   M
　　The universe must have had a cause.

　　　　　mid   M
4. Some atheists are not moral. (M)
　　　　m   mid
　　Renee is an atheist. (m)
　　　　m   M
　　Renee is not moral.

　　　　　mid   M
5. No books of the Bible are in error. (M)
　　　　　mid   m
　　Some books of the Bible are books written by Paul. (m)
　　　　　m   M
　　All books written by Paul are not in error.

　　　　mid   M
6. All men are sinners. (M)
　　　m   mid
　　I am a man. (m)
　　　m   M
　　I am a sinner.

```
      m    mid
7. All S is M.  (m)
   mid    M
   No M is P.  (M)
   m      M
   No S is P.


      m           mid
8. The Bible is the Word of God.  (m)
      mid            M
   The Word of God cannot err.  (M)
      m      M
   The Bible cannot err.


      mid                    M
9. All who have faith in Jesus are saved.  (M)
      m               mid
   Sharon does not have faith in Jesus.  (m)
      m        M
   Sharon is not saved.


      mid                 M
10. Those who obey Christ are believers.  (M)
       m              mid
    Some Christians do not obey Christ.  (m)
       m         M
    Some Christians are not believers.
```

3.2 Validity or invalidity

1. Valid
2. Invalid, illicit minor (Im)
3. Invalid, four terms (4T)
4. Invalid, exclusive premises (EP) (i.e., conclusion drawn from two negative premises)
5. Invalid, undistributed middle (UM)
6. Valid
7. Invalid, weaker premise (WP)
8. Invalid, two affirmative premises/negative conclusion (NC). (This also commits the four-term fallacy, since "have errors" means "are manuscripts that have errors," which is not identical to "errors" in the second premise.)

9. Valid
10. Invalid, UM
11. Invalid, Im
12. Invalid, Illicit Major IM
13. Invalid, 4T
14. Invalid, EP
15. Invalid, (IM)

For 3.1:
1. Valid
2. Invalid, UM
3. Valid
4. Invalid, UM
5. Invalid, Im
6. Valid
7. Valid
8. Valid
9. Invalid, IM
10. Invalid, IM

3.3 Figure

For 3.1:   **For 3.2:**

1. 1   1. 2
2. 2   2. 4
3. 1   3. No figure. A middle term must occur in both premises and not in the conclusion. Syllogisms that commit the four-term fallacy have no middle term. So since figure is determined by placement of the middle term, such syllogisms have no figure.
                 4. 4
4. 1   5. 2
5. 3   6. 1
6. 1   7. 2
7. 1   8. 1
8. 1   9. 2
9. 1   10. 2
10. 1   11. 3
                 12. 1
                 13. No figure. (See #3 above.)
                 14. 1
                 15. 1

3.4 Mood

For 3.1:

1. AAA. ("Not" modifies the terms, not the copulas, in the propositions.)
2. AII (Notice that mood lists major premise first, minor premise second, and conclusion last.
3. AAA

4. OAE
5. EIE
6. AAA
7. EAE
8. AAA
9. AEE
10. AOO

For 3.2

1. EIO

2. AAA

3. EAA (Notice that "Nothing" in the major premise is really "no thing.")
4. EEE
5. AAA
6. EIO
7. OII
8. IAE
9. AEE
10. AAA
11. EAE
12. AEE
13. EAA
14. OEO
15. AEE

3.5 Equivalent sentences

a. Obversion

1. No believers are nonsaved people.
2. Some arguments for God are nonvalid.
3. Jesus Christ is not non-God.
4. All persons are unrighteous (or nonrighteous).
5. Some atheists are not moral (or non-immoral).
6. Morality is not non-universally recognized.
7. No nonbelievers are saved (or non-unsaved).
8. All books of the Bible are inspired (or non-uninspired).
9. Some philosophers are Christians (or non-non-Christians).
10. God is not a non-necessary being.

b. Conversion

1. Some fallen beings are angels.
2. No infallible persons are theologians.
3. Some inerrant things are books in the Bible.
4. None of all the believers is Tom.
5. Not convertible.
6. Some unsaved beings are people.
7. One of the nonbelievers is Tom.

c. Contraposition

1. All equal movements are nonreligions.
2. Some kind people are not believers.
3. Some believers are not non-Christians.
4. Some warranted ideas are not nonbeliefs.
5. All non-invaluable books are non-Bibles.
   Note: "valuable" *is not* the negation of "invaluable."
6. Not contraposable.
7. All non-believers are atheists.
8. Some correct writings are not books not of the Bible (or "nonbooks of the Bible").
9. Intelligent beings are human.
10. Some noncontraposable things are not nonpropositions.

3.6 The Square of opposition

1. a. F
   b. T
   c. F
2. a. F
   b. F
   c. Equivalent, T
3. a. T
   b. Independent, U
   c. T
4. a. U
   b. U
   c. Equivalent, F
5. a. U
   b. U
   c. Equivalent, T
6. a. Independent, U
   b. Independent, U
   c. F

7. a. T
   b. F
   c. T
8. a. F
   b. Equivalent, T
   c. F
9. a. F
   b. T
   c. F
10. a. U
    b. U
    c. T

3.7 For advanced students

1. Invalid, 4T. I call this the "lovers triangle fallacy" and it's a good one to remember. Although it appears to have only three terms, it actually has four. Let's put it in standard logical form:

   > Julie is a lover of Jesus.
   >
   > Paul is a lover of Julie.
   >
   > Paul is a lover of Jesus.

   See the four terms: "Julie," "lover of Jesus," "Paul," and "lover of Julie." Be careful of those missing copulas!

2. Invalid. Obvert the first premise to "No atheists are believers." The resulting syllogism is Figure 1 and mood AEE (notice which premise has the major term). That mood is never valid in that figure. This is the fallacy of Illicit Major because the major premise does not tell us that all who go to heaven are believers.

3. Invalid. Using the square of opposition, and given that the first proposition (I) is true, then the second proposition (O) is undetermined. Since the argument is claiming the second proposition is true, based *only* on the first proposition, it is invalid. This particular invalidity is called illicit subcontrary.

4. Valid. "Not" is modifying the predicate term "guilty" in the minor (second) premise and not the copula. It was established as part of the middle term in the major premise.

5. Invalid, IM. Obvert the first premise.

6. Valid. Same as #4.
7. Valid. Use the square of opposition again.
8. Invalid, Im. The first premise is an exclusive statement. Go back to 2.6 #8 if you need a refresher on exclusive statements.
9. Valid. This falls under the category of a weaker conclusion. (Caution: in some texts this would be considered invalid due to the "existential fallacy." However, this doesn't concern us in this text.)
10. Valid. A really tricky one. First, remember that "flammable" and "inflammable" mean the same thing and can be treated as the same word. Second, you want to avoid changing the conclusion, so always hold it off to last. If you contrapose both premises, you'll see the light.

Chapter 4

4.1 Hypothetical syllogisms
1. G ⊃ M
   M
   ∴ G Invalid, Affirming the Consequent (AC)
2. ~C ⊃ L
   ~(~C)
   ∴ ~L Invalid, Denying the Antecedent (DA)
3. B ⊃ I
   B
   ∴ I Valid, Modus Ponens (MP)
4. C ⊃ S
   S
   ∴ C Invalid, AC
5. E ⊃ ~S
   ~(~S)
   ∴ ~E Valid, Modus Tollens (MT)
6. ~R ⊃ D
   ~D
   ∴ ~(~R) Valid, MT
7. C ⊃ ~T
   ~C
   ∴ ~(~T) Invalid, DA

8. A ⊃ V
   A
   ∴ V Valid, MP
9. C ⊃ N
   C
   ∴ N Valid, MP
10. G ⊃ M
   M
   ∴ G Invalid, AC

4.2 Disjunctive syllogisms

1. E ∨ ~E
   ~(~E)
   ∴ E Valid
2. R ∨ ~G
   R
   ∴ G Invalid, Affirmed the Alternant (AA)
3. G ∨ E
   E
   ∴ ~G Invalid, AA
4. U ∨ ~E
   ~(~E)
   ∴ U Valid.
5. F ∨ U
   F
   ∴ U Invalid, AA

4.3 Dilemmas

1. (T ⊃ H) · (~T ⊃ L)
   T ∨ ~T
   ∴ H ∨ L Valid, Constructive Dilemma (CD)
2. (A ⊃ ~M) · (T ⊃ M)
   ~M ∨ M
   ∴ A ∨ T Invalid, AC
3. (G ⊃ U) · (N ⊃ I)
   G ∨ N
   ∴ U ∨ I Valid, CD
4. (B ⊃ J) · (~J ⊃ ~H)
   B ∨ ~H
   ∴ J ∨ ~J Invalid, Affirmed one consequent
5. (E ⊃ ~P) · (E ⊃ ~B)
   ~(~P ∨ ~B)
   ∴ ~E Valid, Destructive Dilemma (DD)

6. $(M \supset L) \cdot (L \vee G)$
   $L \vee \sim L$
   $\therefore M \vee \sim G$ Invalid, Denied one consequent
7. $(G \supset N) \cdot (\sim G \supset I)$
   $G \vee \sim G$
   $\therefore N \vee I$ Valid, CD
8. $(J \supset F) \cdot (J \supset M)$
   $\sim(F \vee M)$
   $\therefore \sim J$ Valid, DD
9. $(A \supset C) \cdot (B \supset T)$
   $C \vee T$
   $\therefore A \vee B$ Invalid, AC
10. $(C \supset A) \cdot (R \supset B)$
    $\sim(A \vee B)$
    $\therefore \sim(C \vee R)$ Valid, DD

4.4 Refutations of valid dilemmas

1. If one accepts the Bible as true, this dilemma cannot be overcome. If one does not accept the Bible, then you might be challenged to take the dilemma by the horns and challenge the first premise or counter with a another dilemma, like purgatory for example. You can't go through the horns on this one.

3. You also cannot go through the horns here because there is no third alternative. However we can grasp the horns and challenge the first premise. The usefulness of a syllogism is determined by the inference between the premises drawn in the conclusion. A valid conclusion will indeed have information from both premises, but it will not have merely that.

5. The major premise can be denied because it is possible that an omnibenevolent and omnipotent God can use evil in order to achieve a higher good, or he may create free creatures who can freely choose to do evil.

7. It's obvious that we've exhausted the logical possibilities of the second premise, so we cannot go through the horns. The only way you could challenge the first premise is to deny that God is necessary, and propose that he is merely possible (it would be pretty tough to show his existence is impossible). Some today do just that; their theory is called process theology. However that both denies the Bible as literally true and brings in

a lot of other logical problems. Except for that possibility, this dilemma is not overcomable.

8. We can take this one right by the horns and affirm that it is not necessary to Christ's deity that he either fulfill prophecy or do miracles. He would be just as divine if a prophecy were never given of him or if he never performed a miracle. Although once prophecies were given he had to fulfill them, they are only signs to us of his deity, not necessary conditions of it.

10. The major premise here is too vague to warrant any conclusion. What is meant by terms like "regularly," "grow spiritually," and "vindicates"? Until we can get a tighter grip on the meaning of these terms and the verifiability of them, no conclusion follows validly.

4.5 Enthymemes

1. Supply the missing premise: Breaking the law and blocking the doors of abortion clinics saves lives.

2. Supply the missing conclusion: Therefore, Jesus Christ was sent by God.

3. Invalid. The missing conclusion (Therefore Christianity is of God) does not follow because the resulting syllogism commits the four-term fallacy. "Will die out" is future tense and so does not mean the same thing as "has (not) died out."

4. Valid. Major: Some believers will suffer loss at the judgment seat of Christ.
   Minor: All believers are ones who will be saved.
   Conclusion: Some who will be saved are ones who will suffer loss at the judgment seat of Christ.

5. This can be reworded without changing the meaning, and then add the missing premise: Whatever started all this must exist, God started all this, therefore God must exist. In doing enthymemes, some rewording is allowed (and even necessary) as long as there is no significant change in meaning.

6. Supply the missing conclusion: Therefore, Bultmann is not a Christian.

7. Invalid. There is no argument here.

8. This is kind of tricky and can best be placed in a hypothetical syllogism:

210 Come, Let Us Reason

Come, Let Us Reason

If, as deism teaches, God does not intervene in the world, then Jesus Christ is not God. However, Jesus Christ is God. (i.e. it is not true that Jesus Christ is not God.) Therefore, God does intervene (does not not intervene) in the world (and deism is false). Since we have denied the consequent, this is a valid syllogism.

9. Invalid. You will end up with either illicit major or undistributed middle (or both).
10. Supply the missing premise: "Everything complexly designed is created by intelligence."

4.6 Sorites

1. Invalid, IM.
2. Invalid, UM.
3. Valid.
4. Invalid. A key help to remember is whenever you have two negative premises or two particular premises in a sorites, it will be invalid. This one has both!
5. Valid. The first premise is superfluous, but the conclusion follows validly from the remaining premises (Figure 1, Mood EAE). An argument that validly proves its conclusion from some of its premises is not made invalid by the presence of superfluous premises (which of course must not contradict the relevant premises).
6. Valid.
7. Valid.
8. Valid. See #5 for explanation.
9. Invalid, IP.
10. Valid.

Chapter 5

5.1 Mixed syllogisms.

1. Disjunctive, Valid.
2. Categorical, Invalid, Illicit Minor.
3. Destructive Dilemma, Valid.
4. Categorical, Invalid, UM.
5. Hypothetical, Invalid, Denying the Antecedent.
6. Sorites, Invalid, IM, UM (3 and 4), WP.
7. Constructive Dilemma, Valid.

8. Categorical, Valid. This argument best translates to:
   All men are people loved by God.
   All men are sinners.
   Some sinners are people loved by God.
   (Notice that "sinners" in the conclusion is undistributed.)
9. Hypothetical, Invalid, AC.
10. Conjunctive, Valid.
11. Categorical, Invalid, IM.
12. Dilemma, Invalid, AC.
13. Categorical, Valid.
14. Sorites, Valid.
15. This looks like a disjunctive syllogism that is invalid because it affirms one alternant. In reality, the first premise is superfluous, and the conclusion follows validly from the one remaining premise because of the law of non-contradiction, since having a cause and being uncaused are contradictory.
16. Categorical, Invalid, UM.
17. Hypothetical, Valid.
18. Categorical, 4T.
19. Hypothetical, Invalid, DA.
20. Categorical, Invalid, Im.
21. Disjunctive, Valid.
22. Hypothetical, Invalid, AC.
23. Constructive Dilemma, Valid.
24. Categorical, Invalid, Illicit Major (IM).
25. Dilemma, Invalid, AC.
26. Categorical, Valid.
27. Conjunctive, Invalid, Affirming one Conjunct.
28. Sorites, Valid.
29. Hypothetical, Invalid, DA.
30. Disjunctive, Invalid, Affirming one Alternant (AA).

Chapter 6

6.1 Informal fallacies
1. Faulty Dilemma.
2. Appeal to Ignorance.
3. Hasty Generalization.

Come, Let Us Reason

4. Category Mistake.
5. Ad Populum.
6. Special Pleading.
7. Prestige Jargon.
8. Irrelevant Conclusion.
9. Genetic Fallacy.
10. Appeal to Age.
11. Slippery Slope.
12. Equivocation.
13. Begging the Question.
14. Dicto Simpliciter.
15. Appeal to Authority.
16. Faulty Analogy.
17. Complex Question.
18. Ad Hominem (Abusive).
19. Straw Man.
20. Cliche Thinking.
21. Fallacy of Composition.
22. Appeal to Force.
23. Consus Gentium.
24. Faulty Dilemma.
25. Argument of the Beard.
26. Appeal to Ignorance.
27. Irrelevant Conclusion.
28. Appeal to Pity.
29. Begging the Question.
30. Category Mistake (jumping is a process not a place).
31. Slippery Slope.
32. Hasty Generalization.
33. Ad Populum.
34. Appeal to Future.
35. Appeal to Authority.
36. Begging the Question.
37. Red Herring.
38. Dicto Simpliciter.
39. Complex Question.
40. Fallacy of Division.
41. Faulty Analogy.
42. Amphiboly.
43. Ad Hominem (Circumstantial), Genetic.
44. Hypothesis Contrary to Fact.

45. Genetic Fallacy.
46. Consensus Gentium.
47. Cliche Thinking.

Chapter 7

1. Major term: Employee of the university
   Minor term: Member of the organization
   Middle term: One who is present today
   Everyone present today is an employee of the university.
   Every member of the organization is present today.
   Thus, every member of the organization is an employee of the university.
2. Major term: U.S. Citizen
   Minor term: Bill
   Middle term: Voter
   All voters are U.S. citizens (only U.S. citizens are allowed to vote).
   Bill is a voter (Bill has his voter registration card).
   Therefore, Bill is a U.S. citizen.
3. Major term: "A" students
   Minor term: Successful people
   Middle term: People with above-average intelligence
   All "A" students are people with above-average intelligence.
   All successful people are people with above-average intelligence.
   Therefore, all successful people are "A" students.
   Invalid, UM
4. Major term: Wide readership
   Minor term: Decent newspapers
   Middle term: Sensationalism
   All newspapers with wide readership are newspapers that print sensational items.
   No decent newspapers are newspapers that print sensational items.
   Therefore, no decent newspapers are newspapers with wide readership.
5. Modus Ponens
   If the God of the Bible is all-powerful and all-good He will defeat sin.

The God of the Bible is all-powerful and all-good.
Therefore, God will ultimately defeat sin.

6. Modus Tollens
    If a thing could be the efficient cause of itself it would
    have to have been prior to itself.
    But nothing can be prior to itself.
    Therefore, a thing cannot be the efficient cause of itself.

7. Disjunctive Syllogism
    Either Bill scored the last touchdown or John scored the
    last touchdown.
    John did not score the last touchdown.
    Therefore, Bill scored the last touchdown.

8. Major term: Interpreter
    Minor term: News reporter
    Middle term: Interpretative selection
    Every news reporter is someone involved in interpreta-
    tive selection of events to report.
    Everyone involved in interpretative selection is an inter-
    preter.
    Therefore, every news reporter is an interpreter.

Chapter 8

8.1 Averages: mean, mode, median

1. Mean: 30.9
    Mode: None
    Median: 23

2. Mean: 27.4
    Mode: 6
    Median: 6

3. Mean: 1506.25
    Mode: 2000
    Median: 1700; when there is an even number of items
    in the series, the median is the mean of the two middle
    items.

4. Mean: 86.8
    Mode: 86
    Median: 86

5. Mean: $51,404.76
    Mode: $35,000
    Median: $40,000

8.2 Weak and strong inductive arguments
1. Weak, not enough persons involved.
2. Strong.
3. Weak, not carefully examined.
4. Weak, not representative of the country.
5. Weak, contradicts known information.
6. Strong.
7. Weak, not enough time and care.
8. Strong.

8.3 Types of certainty
1. Logical certainty.
2. Existentially undeniable.
3. Inductive certainty.
4. Moral certainty.
5. Virtual certainty.
6. Inductive certainty.
7. Moral certainty.
8. Virtual certainty.
9. Logical certainty.
10. Existentially undeniable.

8.4 Determining probabilities
1. 1 out of 30
2. $1/6 \times 1/6 \times 1/6 \times 1/6 = 1$ out of 1296
3. $4/52 \times 3/51 \times 2/50 \times 1/49 = 24$ out of 6,497,400 or 1 out of 270,725
4. $3/12 = 1$ out of 4
5. $6/30 \times 5/29 \times 4/28 \times 3/27 \times 2/26 \times 1/25 = 720$ out of 427,518,000 or 1 out of 593,775
6. 1 out of 2; this is a common mistake called the Gamblers Fallacy. The probability factor doesn't add up for independent events.
7. 1 out of 31,102; the numbers of books and chapters has nothing to do with the answer, only the number of verses.
8. $3/12 \times 2/11 = 6/132$ or 1 out of 22
9. Possible numbers in an exchange: 10,000
   Total possible number of exchanges: 729
   Total possible numbers w/o area code: 7,290,000
   Total possible numbers in US and Canada: 947,700,000
10. $1/30 \times 1/29 \times 1/28 \times 1/27 \times 1/26 \times 1/25 = 1/427,518,000$

Chapter 9

1. a. The datum to be explained was the unusual orbital path of Uranus, which could not be accounted for by known heavenly bodies.
   b. The hypothesis was the existence of another planet outside the orbit of Uranus.
   c. One method employed in the investigation was the method of residues, the process of eliminating all those stars that did not exhibit the characteristics of a planet, and arriving at the identification of the one that did.

2. a. The datum to be explained is the discovery that after a certain period of time a virulent virus left in a culture was found to have lessened in virulence.
   b. The hypothesis was that there was a relationship between the amount of time the culture was allowed to stand and the relative virulence of the virus.
   c. Pasteur employed the method of concomitant variation. The relative virulence of the virus varied proportionately with the amount of time the culture was allowed to stand.

3. a. The datum to be explained is the historical record of imperialism practiced by capitalistic nations.
   b. The hypothesis is that capitalism is the cause of imperialism.
   c. The hypothesis is invalidated by the use of the method of agreement. In this case, history demonstrates that the effect, imperialism, is often present without the assumed cause, capitalism.

4. a. The data to be explained are the outward signs that seem to indicate that animals are indeed dreaming and the data derived from the EEG.
   b. The hypothesis is that animals, at least the Rhesus monkey, actually dream.
   c. The hypothesis is tested by experimentation and employs the method of agreement. However, the findings are not conclusive because the experimentation has not excluded other possible causes. The conclusion involves some causal fallacies that will be discussed in the next chapter.

Chapter 10

1. Post hoc fallacy. The reading or not reading of one's horoscope has not been demonstrated to be the cause of the success or failure of crops. The arguer is assuming a causal relationship simply on the basis of temporal relationship.

2. Post hoc fallacy. The actions of the Supreme Court may well have been a factor in the rise of the crime rate, but this arguer is concluding a causal relation merely on the basis of temporal relation. Further study must be done and other factors must be considered before any degree of causal relation can be established.

3. Post hoc fallacy. The landlord is concluding that his tenant is the cause of problems simply because the problems did not start until this particular tenant moved in, i.e., a temporal relation. The landlord must take into consideration many other factors, such as the age of the unit, the severity of recent weather, etc., before he can accuse the tenant of being the cause of these problems.

4. Emphasis on irrelevant factors. The implication is that the crisis was the fault of the current administration, and, if Mr. Nixon were to be elected, this kind of thing would not happen. Mr. Nixon overemphasized a single factor that may not have played a part in the cause of the incident at all.

5. Neglect of negative evidence. The arguer has neglected to consider many other factors relevant to the desirability of flying over other means of transportation, such as the increased speed of travel enabling the traveler to reach his destination sooner, the relative infrequency of plane accidents per mile traveled as compared to car accidents, etc.

6. Fallacy of neglecting differences. The arguer has not considered the fact that a similarity in effect does not necessitate an identity of cause. Perhaps the continued rise of the national debt results from the momentum of the economic and political machinery that was set in motion in past years, and the present administration can only hope to slow down the growth. Maybe the policies

of a Democratic Congress contribute to the deficit. Perhaps the debt would have been much higher than it is without the efforts of the Republican administrations. At the very least, it has not been demonstrated that the policies of the recent administrations are the cause of continued growth. The arguer has committed the fallacy of neglecting differences.

7. Fallacy of neglecting differences. The arguer has not considered the fact that similarity of effect does not necessarily indicate identity of cause. It is quite possible that John developed his doctrine of the Logos from the teaching of the Old Testament rather than from Greek philosophy. At least, such an identity of cause cannot merely be asserted. Rather, it must be demonstrated historically, theologically, philosophically, etc.

8. Fallacy of reversing the cause and effect. It is quite possible that this program is the cause of the success of these graduates. However, it is equally possible that those who went on to be successful business executives initially chose the program because they already possessed the necessary skills, and it was the latent skills of these individuals that caused their success. The question is, which is the cause and which is the effect? Is the program the cause of the skills of these former students, or were the latent skills of these individuals the cause of the apparent success of the program?

9. Fallacy of reciprocal causality. This is the fallacy of reciprocal causality. Perhaps causality in this case is not one-directional. Perhaps the two factors feed each other, and as morality drops, pornography is more accessible due to a lessening of the social stigma. Perhaps the growth in the pornography industry has contributed to the relaxing of moral standards. In this case, it may be incorrect to assume a one-directional causal relationship.

10. Fallacy of confusing cause and condition. Although a personal conviction, like belief in God or belief that there is no God, may be a condition in which much inhumanity occurs, it is not the cause of this evil. Individual acts of inhumanity and evil may be caused by political aspiration, greed, hatred, etc., all of which may

be operative in the mind of someone who demonstrates deeply held convictions about God and who wrongly attacks and hurts others in the defense of or the propagation of his convictions. The cause is not the conviction itself. The cause is the individual who endeavors to defend or propagate his convictions in an evil manner.

Subject Index

Scripture Index